The Principal's Chair

The Principal's Chair

Who Sits There Matters, A Secret of School Success

Dr. Judith D. Knotts

ISBN: 1507589352
ISBN 13: 9781507589359

Also available by this author:

Growing Wisdom, Growing Wonder

Elizabeth Gregg and Judith Knotts

(New York: Macmillan Publishing Company, Inc., 1980)

To school administrators who showed me what to do and not do if I wanted to be a principal, who truly made a difference in the lives of students, parents, faculty, and staff—rallying everyone in the community toward excellence.

To aspiring school heads, novice principals, principals in new settings, and savvy school leaders who are always seeking ways to improve: may you glean wisdom from those who have gone before you, inspiring you to be the best you can be.

Our chief want is someone who will inspire us to be what we know we could be.

—Ralph Waldo Emerson

Table of Contents

Launching a New Principal

In your classes and in discussions with colleagues and professors, you have, no doubt, been inspired by the whole-child approach and the power of differentiated instruction, steeped in curriculum content, mapping, and alignment, and saturated by the focus on data analysis of standardized testing for future planning of student success. No matter your age or prior experience (or lack thereof), you are presumed to have a sophisticated grasp of child development and the most effective and up-to-date methods of disciplining children and ensuring safety. Your course work has prepared you, to some extent, for the complex legal and financial matters of school management, the ever-changing but essential attention needed in human resources, and the challenges in construction or remodeling of facilities. Perhaps you have been advised that you will be responsible for devising a risk-management document, that on your campus you will be considered a safety expert on everything from the pandemic flu to blood pathogens, and that in all situations you will be the go-to person for any sort of crisis management. As if these potentially life-threatening events are not daunting enough, as you step into your new position, you will probably also be hailed as the technology guru who will bring efficiency to the modern schoolhouse, whether this is a strong suit of yours or not. Last but not least, in the day-to-day world of schooling, everyone in the community will expect you to be gifted in addressing situations and offering solutions concerning the three-way tension that frequently exists between student, school, and home.

You need these skills to enter the educational workforce, but they will not make you an exemplary school leader, even combined with an A average in graduate school or a distinctive master's thesis or doctoral dissertation. Why? Because you do not lead alone, and those who work for you and with you can just as easily go their own way once classroom doors are closed. You may think you will be a savvy "walking around" principal, leading by being on the move, observing, and suggesting, but you cannot be in all places at once. Even if you could, teachers, despite their apparent group sensitivity, are entrepreneurs at heart who love the privacy of their own instructional space. Teachers savor a closed door where they can do their own thing, being funny or strict or creative as they see fit. It is their kingdom! They think they know what is best for their students, and sometimes they do—but not always.

Your job is to get everyone focused on the same goals with matching priorities. Myriad agendas of faculty members confuse students, divide schools, and diminish the overall effectiveness of the learning environment.

Then, there are the teachers or staff members in every school who have an ax to grind. For whatever reason—they may have been passed over for a promotion or are unhappy in their personal lives—they are hostile. These folks may be small in number, but they should not be ignored. Naysayers can be powerful in their negativity and can overtly or covertly sabotage your educational goals for the school, if not your entire career. In light of this, your job is to get everyone—the "seen it all, done it all" veterans, the seasoned colleagues, the rookies, and even those who may be loaded for bear—on board with the same philosophy and the same practices. It is not an easy task, but with attention to leadership practices for principals, it will lead to student engagement and achievement.

Nonemployees, those essential members of a school community who can help a school excel or tear a campus apart, can pose similar threats to principals as well. A principal may or may not be endorsed by essential players and receive the support of the school board, advisory committees, the PTA, booster clubs, and community organizations and businesses. These unpaid personnel are often a more difficult crowd to win over. As volunteers or interested citizens, they can walk away or, worse yet, cause tremendous turmoil if they are not treated well or are not suitably impressed by the work being done at the school. Sally Helgesen, author and leadership consultant, studied well-run organizations and concurs: "Peter Drucker [the management expert] maintains that the leader of a well-run nonprofit organization [as most schools are] is likely to be more skilled than the CEO of a profit-centered business because the nonprofit manager must rely upon volunteers who will simply devote their time elsewhere if the organization seems troubled." Thus, for schools to be places of excellence where student learning is palpable, the principal needs to possess the personal resources to lead faculty, staff, and volunteers, inspiring everyone to be the best they can be for the good of the students, the school, and the community.

Using This Book

The organization of this book is intended to guide administrators through the journey of leading a school by focusing on the attitudes, behaviors, and practices that can make-or-break a commitment to educational excellence. The text can be read cover to cover or sections can stand alone to inform. Novice principals or seasoned school heads in a new setting will benefit from this intentional approach.

Chapter 1 Beginning the Leadership Journey

For a new school leader or an experienced leader heading to a new school, there is an incredible opportunity to begin the journey in a manner that will promote success. Much of what is done these first months dictates the future. Within four general headings: *Mulling Over What's Ahead, Getting Underway, Taking Specific Steps,* and *Remembering Key Concepts* theory and practice will be explored.

Chapter 2 Doing What Needs to Be Done

The principal is most likely eager to jump in after a brief acclimation period. In this chapter, discussion and suggestions will guide the steps of an intentional leader using four paths to consider: *Deciding What to Do, Determining How to Get Things Done, Gearing Up for the Job,* and *Hanging Tough during the Process.*

Chapter 3 Cultivating Humility While Charging Ahead

Negotiating this delicate balance can be tricky. A leader has to move forward with energy and enthusiasm while keeping a perspective on the whole and reining in an ego. Extraordinary leaders manage to be humble while leading, which undoubtedly contributes to their accomplishments. A purposeful school leader can learn to cultivate humility by absorbing the concepts contained in the four sections: *Realizing People Matter, Working on One's Self, Opening Up to Possibilities,* and *Leading by Serving.*

Chapter 4 Bringing Out the Best in Faculty and Staff

The ultimate test for a leader is to be able to inspire others to perform with passion at maximum proficiency. If students are to become educated citizens able to contribute to society, they need schools that help them reach their potential and make them feel they belong to something bigger than themselves. Teachers and staff members are the ones who make this happen or not. The school leader can learn how to bring out the best in others by reflecting upon the material in four categories: *Creating a Culture, Connecting with Employees, Caring about Colleagues,* and *Changing Minds and Hearts.*

Chapter 5 Keeping Centered in a Chaotic World

The best-laid plans are only the beginning of an arduous journey. A leader must be flexible, comfortable with ambiguity, and able to stay centered in a world that is constantly changing. To be a successful school leader, the following topics need to be examined: *Anticipating Hurdles, Becoming Self-Aware, Masterminding an Approach,* and *Acting with Intention.*

Chapter 6 Flexing Ethical Muscles

Leaders are expected to be ethical; it goes with the territory. People somehow expect more of principals, and they should; school leaders, along with parents, are responsible for preparing the next generation, and actions speak louder than words. The four sections of this chapter: *Setting a Personal Compass, Using a Compass to Guide Relationships, Adopting an Ethics and*

Integrity Policy, and *Employing Ethical Practices* will help principals navigate through the waters that await them.

Chapter 7 Honoring the Leadership Position
Being asked to serve as a school leader should inspire awe. A wise person considers what it means to be in this post and then strives to be true to the calling. The four sections of this final chapter: *Accepting the Role, Looking Inward, Exemplifying Best Practices,* and *Grasping the Essence* should steer important discussions in the classroom and spark soul-searching of the practitioner in private.

One

Beginning the Leadership Journey

MULLING OVER WHAT'S AHEAD

This journey may begin with the very first leadership position in a school, or it may be the beginning of any number of leadership positions in different schools. In the past, principals and superintendents tended to remain in a post for an entire educational career. Today, the tenure of educators in one location is remarkably short; ten years would be considered unusual. A school leader will have the opportunity to begin again and again in a variety of school settings—each one demanding, each one unique, and each one a gift.

Whether you as a new principal are moving across town or across the country, once you sign the contract, your head will be swimming with random details that are mostly concrete and practical—"How shall I set up my office?" "Where are my diplomas?" These nesting instincts are normal and initially helpful. They give you time and space to adjust to your new role before you have to address the nagging, less concrete, but more important, ideas that are floating around in your brain. When you arrive on campus, certain things will jump out at you: the parking lot needs to be repaved, the halls seem dark, and there is no one there to welcome you. You realize that, while these things are relevant, this is not where you should begin… but where do you begin, you wonder? How do you take this place and turn it into a school where students are energized? How do you use the talents of the adults in this community to support children as they explore academics, athletics, and the arts? How do you put all of your theories about learning into some palatable package for everyone to swallow? How do you handle all of the details of the job—getting estimates for resurfacing the parking lot, checking the candle power of the hall lights, and creating a mentor program for new employees—without losing your grip on the overarching issues of delivering a quality education? This is the essential question for school heads—and for all leaders, for that matter. How do you find the balance between the big ideas that need to be discussed and the little things that just have to get done? How do you align lists of things to do for the present and the future?

Before you jump into things, be sure that you have become associated with a school that seems to be the right fit. There are many kinds of schools: public, charter, private, nondenominational, faith-based, special-needs, and unique-mission-driven schools. The worst mistake a principal can make is to sign on with a school that is philosophically incompatible. The best school administrators are those who truly believe in the school's mission or charter and then seek to embody those qualities. Michael found his calling in a traditional Jesuit preparatory school for boys. Bridget, a former bilingual teacher, was most comfortable leading a diverse student body in an urban public school. Kara, a Navajo/Lakota Native American, taught behaviorally disordered middle-school students and later became the founding principal of a charter school for Native Americans. Know who you are before you sign up blindly to serve others. Besides knowing who you are, know who your boss is. This may seem ridiculously simpleminded, but a principal or head of school may be battered from individual to individual and group to group with various people applying pressure, so it is prudent to keep this in mind. A principal and a supervisor usually agree upon goals. Beware of other agendas muddying the waters that can get you off track.

When you arrive, you must fall in love with your school. This is the only way to ensure any measure of success as a school head. "Ho-hum" principals who come to work each day without passion for the place and the people will fail. Without divulging your secret to anyone, you must make this school yours. Of course, you will never mouth the words "my school," which sounds pretentious, but in your heart, you must feel love for the place. When this happens, work will become a pleasure, and affection will change the way you function. You will notice that the flag in front of the building is fraying and will promptly see that it is replaced. You will relish getting the achievement-test scores back, not in a panic mode but with an urge to plan for the future. You will wake up each morning refreshed and eager to see how the day will unfold at school. You may think that your passion is private; it isn't! Teachers, staff members, parents, and especially students always detect when a principal is in love with the place. It's great for everyone when it happens; it's contagious—motivating teachers and staff members to want do their best work, parents to want to lend a hand, and students to want to learn.

In addition to falling in love with your school, show enthusiasm for the locale. As a principal, you may be working in a geographical area that you know and relish, so this will be painless. Or you may be headed to areas that are unfamiliar. The first step in leadership here is to embrace the environment. It may not be easy at first. You may miss mountain peaks or ocean breezes. You may long for the foods you favor. You may not know your way around this strange city. Buck up—you have to become a pioneer and explore the terrain for wonderful new vistas and experiences. Those in your school community want you to love their local parades and their style of pizza; they are proud of these things. Food, festivals, history, natural wonders, arts, commerce, transportation, parks, political personalities, colleges, and athletic teams are just some of the important things in a community that you must learn to appreciate. It may take time. When you are not stuck in the past and seem genuinely eager to get to know this place, however, you will be accepted and supported by the community. Without this enthusiasm and eventual support from the natives, you will fall flat.

GETTING UNDERWAY

When you begin a leadership journey, many eyes will be on you. Comments such as "What does he look like?" "Why did he say that?" or "Why did she change that?" will swirl around you. In this initial period, you are setting the stage for success, mediocrity, or failure. If you ease into the community, you will have a chance. If you come in like a steamroller and flatten everyone and everything in your path, they will eventually drive you out of town. If you seem too passive, they will wonder if you are a true leader. If you bluster about ignoring others, you will lose respect and any chance for enlisting followers. Even though you want to fly in like Superman with your cape flowing and make everything all right in the school, which may be admirable, it is not prudent. Hold off from making major changes during the first year unless the school is brand new, is on "warned status," or is dangerously unsafe.

Most principals enter a school that has none of these special characteristics, and, therefore, a year of watching and waiting is wise before making any sweeping changes. Take this time to figure out what is going on at the school. Who are the movers and shakers? You want them on your side. What is the culture, the "way we do business around here" that is present but not explicitly stated? What are the strengths that must be sustained and the weaknesses that must be addressed? What are the "sacred cows" that you dare not touch? In one East Coast private school with a century of tradition weighing it down, it was an ancient, mossy-green velvet curtain that was balled up and stored in a cardboard carton for the bulk of the year, but on one special day when the middle school presented the Christmas program, the very worn but beloved curtain had to be hung at the gym entrance. To ignore this symbol for the community would have been a major faux pas for the principal. In a Southwest school that was barely a year old, the students proudly recited the Texas pledge each morning. The incoming school head could sense quickly that even though this school was young, this ritual never could be retired. When a new principal arrives on the scene and is respectful of the existing programs and procedures for a time, the members of the community relax a bit. Familiar ways are honored, and people feel safe.

After a solid year of observing and trying to feel the pulse of the school, needed changes can begin in earnest in year two. This is not to say that any critical changes affecting safety, security, or instruction must wait. You just want to be sure you understand the issues, have a clear vision for the school with well-thought-out strategies, and that you have the backing of stakeholders in order for the plans to work.

In the process of gearing up for decision-making, ask questions. When you arrive on campus, or, for that matter, in your position at *any* time, questions are often more important than answers. You are always trying to understand what is before you. People who assume they have all the answers have usually forgotten to begin with the questions. In your probing, ask more open-ended questions than "yes or no" queries. Your goal is to get at the essence of things. Get people talking, and then sit back and listen attentively. Later, at your leisure, sift through the conversation to crystallize the meaning. Leaders are always trying to get a feel for the landscape of the terrain on which they will be treading.

Find out who is who and who does what. "You can't tell the players without a scorecard" was often repeated by an old sports buff, but it's true. As a principal, you need to get a sense of the people in place and an understanding of their jobs. Organizational charts, job descriptions, and room assignments for employees help in the process. Include supervisory roles, such as superintendents and trustees, in your analysis. Be sure you understand the roles and responsibilities here as well, which should be in writing. Review volunteer posts and committees; find out what they do to benefit the school. Put all of these pieces of the puzzle together so you can see the team as a whole and begin to understand your job as the CEO, the connector of the pieces. Be sure to bond with the leader of the parents' association. This elected officer of the PSA or PTA carries significant clout. She, as is most often the case in schools, can rally her troops to raise needed funds for projects, assemble volunteers in a flash, and be your ally in time of school-wide skirmishes. Don't leave this relationship to chance. Invite her to meet with you as soon as you come on campus, and then have periodic standing meetings to stay in touch. For your part, you can help the association by attending critical meetings and appreciating publicly the work being done by the association that benefits the entire school community.

As you get underway, watch that your personal life does not invade your professional life. Followers do want their leaders to be real with a personal life to complement their careers, but in the office the emphasis has to be on the school. Occasionally, principals move into their new offices armed with family photos that take up every available shelf. One or two personal photos are fine, but what the community really wants to see in the principal's office are student photos—the robotics team that won the state championship, the Brownie troop doing community service at a senior-citizen center, or the current student council. School heads spend their lives dealing with children, and, because this topic is so near and dear to their hearts, it is easy for them to slip into the habit of mentioning their own children's achievement to outsiders. Big mistake. You were not hired because of your personal parenting skills; you were hired as a professional to ensure that all students under your leadership will learn.

Before any specific action is taken, the school community wants to know what's in your head and in your heart. Don't be hesitant to tell them your goals and dreams. This should happen when you first arrive in a school and at the beginning of each school year thereafter. Max De Pree studied leadership and wrote, "The first responsibility of a leader is to define reality." He also said, "A leader paves the way for change." An inexperienced principal—or, worse, a lazy one—keeps faculty, staff, parents, and students guessing what is important, and thus they only find it out when they are caught doing something "wrong." Keep your goals short, simple, and few so adults and children can latch on to something memorable and believe they are doing something "right" for a change. Once you have shared your ideas with the school community, post the yearly goals or the school's mission statement prominently on its website and in print. Your desk, the classrooms, and the front hall should have attractive photocopies displayed so everyone in the building can be reminded of the path when facing decisions; use these as your guides. To further your mission, use the words "colleague," "partnership," "team," "collaborate," and "community" frequently. If you really believe in these concepts and lead with this style, you will see your hopes come to fruition. People need to hook complex ideas on to simple words.

TAKING SPECIFIC STEPS

To be a real leader, you want to run effective meetings from day one on the job. A principal's life seems to move from one meeting to the next sometimes without even a bathroom break, so for those meetings that the principal is leading, it is critical to know how to run them smoothly and to help others learn how to follow suit. Standard meeting times often work well; people keep slots open on their calendars, and it helps a principal ensure that key personnel are met with regularly. Have a printed agenda if possible, start and end on time, and keep attendees on topic. Sometimes this means limiting discussion or roping people back into the topic at hand. Listen for comments that are not really part of the meeting, and nip them in the bud saying something like, "That is an interesting point, Larry. Let's discuss it at a later date and not keep the rest of these folks any longer than we have to." Be sure to get back to Larry, however, so he feels valued. Become adept at handling attendees who want center stage and try to do most of the talking. After a few of these spotlight performances, say, "That is helpful, Lucille. Now I want to hear what everyone else thinks about this." Have a notetaker at meetings, and have notes sent to attendees and to those who were unable to attend. At the end of the meeting, review the topics discussed and any key decisions made or tasks assigned. Remember to thank everyone for his or her time and input.

Next, establish a communication system. People on campus and in the community need to hear from you. The superintendent may send his communications regularly, the classroom teachers may e-mail a weekly news flash to parents, and the PTA may flood the school with flyers about upcoming events—all good things designed to serve students—but these efforts don't get you off the hook. Your school community hungers for your input. They want to know what you care about and what is being done to sustain and improve their school. Not every principal is a born writer but practice helps, and having to put ideas down on paper often crystallizes thoughts. Find your own voice. If you speak with a touch of humor, write with that same touch. If you speak in staccato bursts, write that way. There is nothing worse than an everyman trying to sound like a Shakespeare. Be authentic, but be sure to be heard. It is smart to establish some schedule for your communications, and then people in the community can look forward to your bulletins. For principals who write fairly easily, a weekly communiqué is possible. If you struggle putting words to paper, aim for a biweekly piece. Pick a catchy name for your correspondence so people will begin to discuss it by title and topic. You want a community buzz about this; it helps bring people together. Terry, a dad of two and a transcontinental pilot, said that reading the school's "Messenger" online in Paris or Tokyo made him feel like a part of the community despite the miles separating him from his children and the school. Printing, collating, and postage fees of the past have given way to mass e-mails, so there is no excuse for not doing this. A school head worth his salt is constantly finding ways to connect.

If at all possible, bring on board the best receptionist you can find. This person must personify the welcoming atmosphere you want for the school. She or he must also be efficient and able to work with students, teachers, other staff members, parents, and the public at large. Many little and big problems are solved at this desk. It may be a teary kindergartener who arrives late one day, it may be parents who are estranged and arrive separately for a parent-teacher conference, or it may be someone hoping to sell new team uniforms—all in a day's work for the school receptionist. Calmness, kindness, and discretion are essential traits for this person, and a healthy sense of humor doesn't hurt either. An attentive receptionist can pave the way for a positive meeting with the principal or teacher; a dismissive receptionist can damage the school in ways not imagined. Treat this person with respect and dignity; it is a difficult job—perhaps more so than yours.

A very first step that says much about you and your philosophy is to make your campus and your buildings as inviting as possible. You want children eager to come through the doors and feel that school is special. Other than half-day kindergarten classes, students spend most of their day at school. School buildings don't have to be state of the art, but they do have to be clean, safe, warm or cool as needed, and have adequate space for the number of students served. In one of our major cities, an elementary school had crumbling front cement steps, broken or boarded-up windows, and bathrooms with toilets that did not flush. This school also had dismal achievement scores. Common sense tells us that there was a correlation here. Work with your students, the PTA, and the neighborhood to make the buildings and grounds as attractive as possible. Your district funds or your school budget may not include painting or plantings, so recruit volunteers. A byproduct of this approach is the camaraderie that will develop among the workers. Dismiss any concerns about the viability of this approach with diverse economic populations. At a low-income high school in the Southwest, students painted portable classroom buildings, and at an expensive private school in the East, parents planted trees and bulbs. Both groups were proud of their work and, as a result, felt more connected to the school. One principal who really understood the importance of a welcoming place swept the front walk each morning before greeting the students. This simple gesture said, "I care; we are ready for you; come in and learn about the wonders of the world."

Even though you are just starting, you will want to establish a hiring protocol. In some public-school systems, preliminary screening will be done for you. In other schools, you are completely on your own. Gathering names and résumés from the central office, a hiring firm, or the responses from an ad in the local paper is only the first step. You need to sift through these papers to see who you want to interview. When you or your administrators conduct an interview, allow sufficient time. An hour is usually necessary to scope out a candidate. Sometimes you know in five or ten minutes that this person is not right for the job. He may appear unkempt, she may be late for the appointment, he may not be able to look you in the eye, and she may talk nonstop. These are the easy decisions. The more difficult ones are the candidates who appear at first glance to be OK and they have the requisite credentials.

Now comes the hard part: you need to find out who they are as people. When you hire, you are looking for two things. You want to hire the most qualified person for the job, but you also want a role model, not only for students but also for colleagues and parents. Credentials are usually easier to decipher than personal qualities. Have in your protocol some standard questions that may not appear on a résumé, such as, "What gifts would you bring to this school?" "What brings you joy?" "What three words describe you?" Have an interview sheet in front of you so you can jot down notes as the candidate is speaking. This is not rude; it indicates that you are interested in what is being said.

Interviewing is an art, despite research companies wanting it to be more of a science. You and the candidate are both buying and selling; you each want something, and like Charlie in *Charlie and the Chocolate Factory* you are searching for the "golden ticket." Note the energy and enthusiasm of the candidate. Imagine being a student and spending a day with this person. Would you be inspired or bored to death? What is this candidate's voice tone and pattern of speech? Would you want to listen, or would you be put off by the grating sound and the poor diction? Pay attention to the flow of conversation during the interview session. Is this candidate able to balance speaking and listening, or is it all talk or mostly awkward silences? Does the candidate seem prepared? Has he brought a neat list of reference names and numbers, should it be needed? Has she brought a portfolio so you can gain a sense of her prior experiences without expecting you to go page by page through the binder? If your school is small, this important task is all yours. If your school is large, still be involved and interview the final candidate or candidates your administrators have selected. As principal, you are responsible for each person hired. People make student engagement and achievement happen in schools; honor this by giving the hiring process the time and attention it is due.

Subsequently, check references thoroughly. A school head cannot be careful enough in checking out past employment performances of applicants. As a rule of thumb, get at least two references per applicant. Don't let time pressures eliminate this important step in the hiring process, although you may be tempted to do so a week before school opens when you are still searching for that solid math teacher. Have a standard form that you or a member of your leadership team fills out, including who made the call, who was called, the date, in what capacity the reference knew the candidate, for how long, would the reference person rehire the candidate, what were the candidate's strengths, what were the candidate's weaknesses, and any other information the reference will provide. Ask open-ended questions so you have an opportunity to hear from the reference. "Yes" and "no" queries usually divulge only surface information. If you encounter a reference that refuses to furnish any information beyond the employment dates of the candidate, go back to the candidate and ask for additional references. If you or someone else in school knows the candidate, still follow this system. Teaching second grade is not the same as being a reliable volunteer in the community. Being a middle-school English teacher requires different skills than teaching lacrosse. If you hear any hesitation in the responses of a reference, think twice about hiring this candidate.

REMEMBERING KEY CONCEPTS

Be visible. Find times each day to be seen. Just showing up is a prerequisite for success. You could stand at the front door, shake hands, and say, "Good morning! Have a great day." You could be at the hectic bus-loading lines at the end of the day, bidding everyone a safe trip home. You could be in the front hall welcoming everyone at Back to School Night, saying, "So glad you came." You are the host at all school events and must act accordingly. Principals who sit at their desks all day are either depressed, incurable introverts, or just not aware of how important it is to be seen amid the daily action on campus. School heads that delight in crossing action items off their to-do lists have to learn to write board reports, evaluations, and recommendations after regular school hours when the halls are quieter.

Welcome diversity. Wherever your school is located, your students will learn more about the world and themselves if they are part of a diverse community. In your hiring, look for interesting people who will bring different talents and experiences to the campus. Mary Ann, a principal of a large high school in a university town, had a leadership team that was extraordinary. This unique group of administrators who were Latino, African American, and Caucasian stuck together to get the job done. An "open-arms" approach works with little ones as well. A private primary school in the suburbs worked hard to enable Mary, an English woman with excellent teaching credentials, to come to the States. After some time, things worked out, and Mary brought pieces of her own culture with her to share with the kindergarteners. Get a feel for your school community, and then consider some possible ways to diversify.

Surround yourself with honest, positive people. You may not always have a choice, but keep an eye out for these folks and then nab them for your day-to-day circle of colleagues. Negative people drag you down. You will have to deal with them. However, it can be draining, so limit the number in your life. Although you want positive people in your work life, you also want honest ones. Yes-people who just want to please and who don't tell you what they really think never help you get to the truth.

Avoid favoritism. Regardless of age or experience, the principal is the "parent" in the school community, and everyone in the school family wants to be thought of as special. This is a demanding role because different personalities bring out the best and worst in all leaders. The "likeables" are easy to deal with; they follow the rules, go through the day with a smile, and make you laugh. The prickly ones, on the other hand, make you stretch to find a connection and challenge you to want to help them be the best they can be. Stay in tune with these sometimes ornery folks. They often can be brought along with time and attention, and it may be worth the effort for everyone.

Make plans and then follow up. The best-laid plans are worth nothing if they are left to drift. Implementation requires serious intentionality. School administrators Janet, Misty, and Matt would come to every meeting with a laptops under their arms. They were prepared to research, make to-do lists, and file minutes; this efficiency saved everyone endless hours. When they did not have their trusty laptops, they had to figure out other methods to remember what was expected of them. Christy, a young engineer and business-school grad turned school administrator, surprisingly went non-tech and carried a hardback journal everywhere to record comments, facts, and follow-ups. Find ways that work for you as head of a school to manage the details of leadership. Microsoft Outlook calendars and electronic lists, Post-it Notes, yellow legal pads for each project, or colored files to house notes and reports for topics underway are all possible ways to manage following up. Schedule periodic meetings to assess the progress of specific plans. As the principal, you don't do all of the work, but it is your responsibility to manage the flow and see that things get done.

In your leadership journey, realize that you are leading each step of the way, and many eyes are on you. The student teacher doing her practicum is watching you welcome people into the building and is taking note for her classroom in the future. The janitor is seeing you pick up litter on the way into the building and is feeling a kinship. The basketball coach is hearing you comment on the fine sportsmanship shown at last night's game and is inspired to give his players a similar message. The student council members are observing how you run a meeting with respect, preparation, and effectiveness and are emulating your style. The second-grade class is noticing how you greet the librarian with a smile and a "thank you" and are echoing your words. The teachers are recognizing the dedication you show daily and also are trying to be the best they can be. The school board and superintendent are noticing your energy, self-effacing style, and commitment to student achievement and are supporting your efforts. You are leading all the time.

The first days, weeks, and months are the most important ingredients of a successful leadership journey. Don't drift into a community and expect a red-carpet treatment and open arms from everyone just because you are the principal. People will be watching and waiting to see you in action. Be intentional. Give it your best shot. Well begun is half done.

Two

Doing What Needs to Be Done

DECIDING WHAT TO DO

Before you roll up your sleeves and start making changes as principal, do some serious thinking. Ask yourself the following questions: What needs to be done? How should I go about getting it done? And, most importantly, why do it? Your education, experience, powers of observation, listening skills, and ability to interpret data should jump-start the process of creating a plan. Essentially, you are crystallizing everything you know into a complete package that will ensure learning for all children entrusted into your care. The concrete and obvious needs will be easiest to identify. Other subtle but equally important issues deserve attention—there is a punitive attitude in the school that seems to permeate everything, academics often take a back seat to athletics, and faculty members appear to be going through the exercise of teaching with little enthusiasm. Jot down your impressions and ideas, then hunker down while you keep looking, listening, and analyzing. A good way to grasp issues immediately is to substitute in a class. Step in when there is an emergency need for a sub, not when the teacher, department, or students have time to plan for your visit. There is no better way to see what is going on in a school than to be in the thick of the action. You will notice academic strengths and weaknesses in students. You will discern if discipline procedures are working or not. You will witness student engagement and joy in learning or be disturbed by the apathy in the room. Even seemingly little things will jump out at you that need attention: the announcements are annoying, the hallways are littered with debris, the overhead projector is not working.

When you go about gathering information, be sure to review attendance records. Getting to school is the first step in school achievement. As a student, even if you are smart, you have to be present to get the assignments, hear the lectures, work in groups, master the material, and take tests. Read the policies for attendance and tardiness, and ask if the rules are enforced. Find out why students do not attend regularly (which will vary tremendously), and then plan individual solutions for each student. One size does not fit all. Grace, a high-school student in a large public California school, cut every class but history where she excelled. The teacher discovered this and asked her why. Grace said, "No one ever notices if I am here or not except in this class, so why bother?" The caring history teacher took charge and worked with the principal and the district. Grace was tested and found to be incredibly able and knowledgeable enough to test out of many high-school classes. They helped her attend a local university part time while still a high-school student. From then on she soared, receiving a full college scholarship and eventually becoming a Rhodes Scholar, all because someone noticed that she skipped school and wanted to find out why.

Instead of relying solely on your powers of observation, take the time to get impressions from others in the school. Schedule one-on-one sessions with your key administrators, and ask them to come to the meeting prepared to discuss three things that are working in the school and three things that are not. Meet with student groups and encourage a similar candid dialogue. One new school head scheduled student gatherings in his office throughout the fall and made sure to have random students selected to get a range of ideas and feelings from various grade levels. If you structure these student groups by interest alone, the discussion will be limited to challenges facing the honor society or the basketball team. Have faculty and staff focus groups as well as gatherings for parents to garner opinions on key issues. This is a way to demonstrate inclusivity without bending to any particular party in power. Make it clear that this system is designed for information sharing and not decision-making.

Because it should be obvious that you want to hear from others, you will be flooded with impressions and suggestions, and, therefore, you will have to become adept at identifying critical issues and emerging patterns. When you meet with individuals, try to discern the real meaning behind the conversations. An open-door policy will invite more complaints than kudos, which is to be expected. Your job as the school head is to try and figure out the real issues behind the whining before you jump in and offer solutions. For example, a parent may come to you as a last resort, complaining about a teacher, saying that her child wants to transfer to another math class because her current class is boring and the teacher is inept. Is the issue the child, the parent, or the teacher? This may take some collective digging to figure out the actual problem and the best solution. Be aware also of praises in order to give credit where it is due.

Regardless of your school structure—public, private, or charter—there will be change initiatives coming from the superintendent's office, an accrediting agency, the health or fire department, the diocese, and an advisory board or board of directors, just to mention a few. Certainly you must attend to these directives and include them in your goals and plans. If any of these initiatives are suggestions, rather than directives from the powers that be, make time to consider the advice with the appropriate teams and then get back to the group who issued the report with your response. These decrees alone, while important to attend to, will not create a school of excellence. That is your job. So as your ideas begin to jell, start a to-do list. Some of the changes you have in mind will be data driven, from test scores, attendance profiles, college acceptances, safety and security records, budgets, faculty and staff performance records, and employee-retention statistics. Walking through the campus and listening to exchanges will prompt changes. Other impressions and ideas will just make themselves known; at times it may seem that ideas or solutions will pop out of thin air, making you suspect their validity. Don't second-guess this system. Value your intuition; it is a pretty amazing phenomenon. Past experiences, readings, conversations, and thoughts are stored in our brains, even though we are not aware of their presence. These sensations, concepts, and feelings somehow mingle without our consciously willing the motion, and suddenly strange and wonderful meaning is made. Intuition was once thought to be hogwash, an intellectual failing of the fairer sex, but now psychologist and management experts recognize its value.

When you feel that your goals are well-thought-out, prioritize them. You cannot do everything at once. For those of you who feel more secure with a system to rely on, David Allen, author of *Getting Things Done: The Art of Stress-Free Productivity*, offers a planning model that may be useful. According to Allen, "No matter what the setting, there are five distinct stages that we go through as we deal with our work. We (1) *collect* things that command our attention; (2) *process* what they mean and what to do about them; (3) *organize* the results, which we (4) *review* as options for what we choose to (5) *do.*"

DETERMINING HOW TO GET THINGS DONE

It's a heady feeling to have a to-do list finally in hand. However, before you dive into action, think long and hard about how you will go about getting things on this list done. You may be the major list maker, but you are a minor player in getting all of the tasks accomplished. You need to inspire others and get them to commit to you and your goals, not only with their heads but also with their hearts. Many of the things on your personal to-do list are techniques designed to bring out the best in others so that the ultimate goal of learning can be reached. Dismissing the "how" of getting to success is imprudent and will dictate eventual failure. Throughout the entire process, know why you are making changes and why each item is on your to-do list. You have to be able to answer these questions to your own satisfaction in order to answer these questions convincingly to others.

Management consultant Allen notes that asking why "defines success. It creates decision-making criteria. It aligns resources. It motivates. It clarifies focus. It expands options." As a leader, get into the habit of asking *why* and *how*. It will inform and expand learning opportunities for everyone in the school community.

Another idea about decision-making comes from Kathleen Eisenhardt, a Stanford professor. She believes, " Before you can figure out how to do something, you must first define what you want to do." She further states, "Although defining objectives may seem obvious, they are often—at first, anyway—too vague. Instead, objectives should be precise."

So to become more intentional and specific with your objectives, begin with yourself. Get out of your comfort zone. If you are a football fan and never miss a game, that is fine, but look for other school events that you also need to support in person…a Latin competition, an art show, the drill team. If you are not a sports fan, become one. Have the athletic director keep you abreast of practices and games on campus and drop by several. You don't need to stay for the whole game. Be sure to watch the junior varsity or B teams as well as the varsity stars. If there is one constant complaint on school campuses about a principal, it is that he or she rarely attends a choral concert or an international relations debate. Be among the first to buck this trend.

Historically, many male high-school principals were former physical-education teachers. The thinking was that these men were imposing and could keep order in a school, and, of course, most of them loved sports. While this is still the case in some places, new principals and established principals must do all they can to support all extracurricular activities on campus, not just the big athletic draws. Let your emotional stretching continue. Show your silly side once in a while. Wear pajamas for kindergarten hibernation day, play a bit part in the musical, or sit in the dunking booth at the school fair. Students, faculty, staff, and parents can't help but smile to see their usually staid leader a bit silly, which helps when you have to face more serious things together. By extending yourself to points that at first felt a far reach, you will be growing as a principal. In doing so, you will be discovering things about the school and the people in it that you need to know, and they will be getting to know you.

While you are considering how to get things done and are relishing your role as a "walking around" principal earnestly cataloging every observation, don't just focus on behaviors that need to be changed. Notice goodness. This may sound pointless, but catching a child or an adult doing something good and commenting on it will generate more of that same behavior. This is such an easy way to create the culture you envision. The trick is being honest and specific in your noticing. Don't invent a piece of goodness that isn't really there. To the awkward middle-school boy who is uncomfortable in his size eleven shoes but who stops on his own to help the receptionist carry boxes to her desk, this is a chance to be a knight and for one brief moment get out of his preadolescent egocentric self-conscious shell. If he is noticed, all the better; he will feel honored in his goodness. Become that inspired school head who discerns goodness and affirms it. Tell the receptionist that you admire the way she handled a difficult phone call. Let the coach know that you appreciate the way he greets his players each afternoon with a smile and a nutritious snack he prepared. How unfortunate it would have been to miss this instance of goodness. Recognize group excellence as well, and instill pride in the school that is justified. Acknowledge the football victories and the burgeoning honor society, but don't stop there. Celebrate a clean campus free of debris and graffiti. Commend the community for a lack of violence at school. Praise the cooperative efforts of the PTA. You want to look for opportunities to lift the spirits of individuals and the school community in general.

A good leader is enthusiastic without being overbearing. Even though your main goal as a school head is student engagement and academic achievement, you need to make space for rituals and celebrations. These activities do more than spur achievements and respect traditions. They are the most basic way of bonding a community together. Ideas and victories that are mostly abstract in nature need some kind of concrete expression. Having an honors assembly publicly dignifies student successes in academics, athletics, and the arts. Morning meetings in the classroom, advisory group competitions, volunteer appreciation day, homecoming, field day, and baccalaureate are milestones that help members of the school community know they belong. Belonging begets engagement.

As you discern how to get important things done in your school, surely there is nothing more salient than believing in your students. This includes even the naughty, the academic failures, and the dropouts. They cannot learn if they do not believe it is possible. Vicki, a "force to be reckoned with" principal in an alternative public high school for juniors and seniors, achieved incredible success with students who had failed in more traditional schools. Why? Because she loved them and showed it. She smiled at a teen mother toting a baby into school with her, she hugged a student who just looked needy, and she bragged about all of their talents and successes to anyone who would listen. These former failures began to believe in themselves and when they did, they succeeded. Vicki wasn't a pushover; she had standards and school policies, but she governed with love, and everyone knew it. Thus this school for at-risk students in a run-down neighborhood became known for academic excellence. When children and adults believe that they matter to someone and have a voice in a community, they will be able to rise to the challenge of change.

GEARING UP FOR THE JOB

As much as you long for the go signal, to be a really effective school leader, you must spend even more time now getting ready before you jump into action. Impulsive principals may look formidable at the starting gate and during the initial lap, but their initiatives are rarely sustainable because they have not invested time and effort in building the change platform.

For your goals to be reached, you want to have various systems in place. Start with students; they are the reason the school exists and you have a job there, so make a concerted effort to know them by name. Educational research indicates that one person cannot know more than about 625 persons. Your school size will determine how you manage to connect with children. If you have more than 625 students, which many schools do, your school is probably divided into smaller units. Elaine, headmistress of a public high school in an affluent area, which also served recent immigrants, split her school of more than two thousand into houses so all students could feel they belonged somewhere. This collegiate-inspired system worked well. Each student would be called by name, indicating that someone cared.

Lois, a principal in a middle school of 950 students, was determined to know her students by name and had her own methods. She personally built the master schedule during the summer and placed each student in the Professional Learning Community where that child would get the one-to-one personalization with a staff member who would love him or her, so this principal had a head start once school began. She didn't stop there. Lois was visible in the classrooms daily and would look at seating charts and listen for the teacher or students using names, which helped her memorization. Especially during the first month of school, she was out and about the school by 7:00 a.m., observing groups and chatting with individual students. In her school, there was a high turnover, so each transferred student and family met with her, making it easy to remember these new people. Attending rehearsals, practices, games, and gatherings helped Lois know not only names but also something about each child. She knew that using names validated people, so she made it a priority as a principal. The first year in a school is the hardest. After that, you only have to get to know the hundreds of new students.

Learning names is just step one; you will want to engage student leaders at all levels. Student council, safety patrols, admission ambassadors, peer mediators, and class officers are your right arms in a school community.

Meet with them, honor their work, and help them grow as leaders. They, in turn, will help you grow and manage change.

While you are learning student names, you simultaneously will be thinking about the adults in your professional sphere. Be resolute. Surround yourself with smart, selfless people. Principals need to know a little about a lot of things. During the course of one day, a principal could be expected to address the special needs of an autistic child, the football scoreboard that was hit by lightning, a disciplinary hearing relating to violence on campus, a parent challenging a book on the syllabus for an English class, the choice of playground surfacing material, a newspaper article focusing on students becoming Eagle Scouts, an injury in the cafeteria, or the logic of using a virtual server to help meet the demands for more electronic storage space. Clearly, one person, even the most experienced principal, cannot have a depth of knowledge in all of these areas. Make sure your leadership team has strengths you do not, so together you can deliver a quality educational program to the students.

Continue your efforts and involve other adults. Find the folks on the fringe. When you enter a room or circulate at a gathering, notice those who are standing on the periphery. These are the people whom you have to bring into the fold. Whether they are basically shy, new to the organization, or just feel socially uncomfortable in a group situation, they hold back. A real leader has antennae up at all times looking for ways to help others acclimate and connect. Forget those individuals who are chatting away and always at the center of the action; they rarely need your helping hand. To deliver a quality education to students, you need everyone in the school community to be as engaged as possible. As a professional who is probably accustomed to technology playing a major role in your life, you may be wondering why I am placing so much emphasis on people. Of course, advance school technology as needed to support learning and communication in your community while remembering that no e-mail, blog, or electronic message can substitute for a face-to-face connection with people. Use technology to make your job easier, not harder. Issues of any importance are best served in real meetings if at all possible. Seeing facial expressions and hearing intonations convey the message as much as words do.

Since you are addressing the significance of human capital in the change process, don't hold back. Ask for help. Big men and little ladies are usually the ones who are reluctant to say, "Can you help me?" "Incredible Hulks" hate admitting that they cannot do something alone. They are proud they can bench press three hundred pounds and push a stalled car out of traffic. "Five foot two, eyes of blue" gals want to prove that size does not indicate competence. They haul their own suitcases everywhere and huff and puff quietly as they too refill the water cooler bottles at work. The rest of us show the same characteristics as these two personality types from time to time. We want to be independent, but truthfully, we are often needy. We want to be strong but occasionally feel weak. This is a common conundrum for you as a leader to consider. How do you march ahead with a plan and radiate positive energy while still letting followers know that you are not invincible and need their help? Purpose, passion, and plainspokenness are your best weapons. People may be intrigued by a leader who appears to be a lone ranger, but the fascination is usually short lived, and followers don't personally engage. On the other hand, people are inspired by an honest leader who asks for help. They listen and, if swayed, they will commit.

While gearing up to do what needs to be done, consider some practical steps. Find a sounding board you trust, which can be an invaluable asset for a principal. Ed was a perfect confidant for one school head. He was a terrific listener—sometimes so good that on the phone you had to stop and check on his breathing to know he was still there! He was not a parent in the school, thus he had no personal agenda to push, but, as a parent of three, understood schools. His willingness to take calls was remarkable. He could be at his desk or in the car on the way to a meeting, yet his reassuring voice was always present on the first or second ring, saying, "What's up?" Besides being assured of personal integrity and total confidentiality, you need some sort of long-distance handshake that indicates you will turn to this sounding board, accepting that you may have differing points of view on an issue but will operate with mutual respect. This was one secret of the success between Ed and a school head. They had genuine regard for each other, and they understood and accepted this handshake relationship. In addition to one good advisor with a great ear, create contact lists. You need other people to help you do your job well, and you may find when you least expect it that you could use the help of a police officer or a politician. These names and addresses will come in handy when you want to do a mass mailing for the school. An old-fashioned Rolodex is useful for making quick phone calls, especially if the computer system is down or the power is off. An organized binder of personal cards can help when you are trying to recall someone's title or affiliation. These various lists will grow year by year, and as you remain in the community or in the profession, these may become some of your most valuable tools as an administrator.

Another practical suggestion is to have a crash book. In this age of electronic information, we depend on computers to communicate and store data. School heads that were in Hurricane Katrina's path learned a painful lesson. You cannot always rely on technology when you need it. Many of these people did not have phone numbers, addresses, or critical information at their fingertips when they needed it most. So, to be safe, in addition to the sophisticated systems that house your school information, create a binder that contains all of the information you would need in an emergency. Especially in times of crisis, everyone turns to the principal for information. You need to be sure you have it. All this is part of the vital gearing-up process that precedes actual change.

HANGING TOUGH DURING THE PROCESSS

OK, you're ready to go. So set high standards and mean it. Goals are great when there is oomph behind them. To commit to something takes not only attacking skills but also staying power. A principal has to have a long suit in perseverance. Change takes planning and plodding and people who want to go along for the ride. A high-functioning school where students are achieving regardless of the demographics is one where there is an energetic leader with purpose and passion and is full of people who want to be part of the place. Successful leaders on any front learn to work forward and backward simultaneously. As a school head, with your to-do list in hand, think of where you want the school to be in the future and then work backward and develop a very specific timeline of how to make this happen. Monthly, weekly, and daily parcels of the task should be defined for you and the implementation team. Often good ideas stagnate because this system is ignored. Principals have to be master timekeepers without seeming unduly militant. Another delicate balance is required. You must be willing to delegate tasks, for there are always colleagues more competent in specific areas than you are; moreover, you do not have the time or energy to do everything.

On the other hand, you must assume your fair share of responsibility beyond your role as delegator. Carl was thought to be a wonder boy when he first arrived at a school. He took charge with a firm hand and within weeks reassigned most of his responsibilities to other administrators, staff members, and teachers. Initially, it seemed like this was going to be a brand-new, streamlined school operation bound for success, however, after a while it became apparent that Carl had little involvement in the day-to-day operations while other folks were becoming overburdened. He was not viewed as team player, nor was he feeling like a team member despite his cheery "Go, team, go" demeanor. Your colleagues need to see you do some of the heavy lifting, and, like them, you need to feel the frustration working through an assignment and relishing the exhilaration when it is completed.

Watch calendars as well. When the principal does not adhere to agreed-upon due dates, everyone else feels there is a lot of wiggle room for completion of projects, and important tasks do not get done in a timely manner.

This is more than an inconvenience for the person managing the project. Tardiness can affect accreditation, grants, high-school and college admissions, publications, audits, schedules, and more.

Change is omnipresent in a school and requires steeliness and sensitivity in its leader. You have to be able to face the difficult discussions that come before you. Shying away from an awkward or painful situation is not the mark of a courageous leader. Telling a counselor in a suburban elementary school that her diamond nose stud would distract young students and informing a transplanted Brit that his use of the words "bloody hell" was not acceptable language in an American school were conversations that had to be held for the good of the employee as well as the students. You also have to learn to say "no" politely. It is so much easier being the nice guy and saying "yes" all the time, but that is not the function of a school head. Your job is to make sure that instructional time is sacred and that learning is the top priority. Even with teachers, this mission sometimes gets misplaced. They too will want to please their students or a school group, and they will be willing to let academics take a back seat. Principals who are personally and professionally secure are able to say "no" to the fifth-grade teachers who want to plan a field trip to the amusement park, to the chorus that wants to do a car wash last period to raise funds for a competition, or to the PTA group that wants to announce the bake sale over the loudspeaker—all perfectly good intentions, but not appropriate during the school day. In general, think about eliminating all school-wide announcements. Regardless of when announcements are given, some important instructional time is lost. Use the school-wide sound system only for emergencies and not daily announcements.

Being sensitive as a school head means understanding the possible ramifications of positions taken, so don't just send out a change order and expect compliance. Anticipate reactions. When you realize that your decisions affect lives, you will begin to take time to think about the possible reactions to your mandates. This doesn't mean waffling when you consider the possible flak you will be getting; it just means being prepared. Do your homework, and be ready to deliver logical explanations, possibly a second and third time if necessary. You can't please everyone; some people will clap their hands in delight with your decision while others will curse you quietly.

In gearing up for the job, remind yourself that doing what needs to be done requires courage. Beware of anxiety, the demon behind procrastination. Of course, you and others will make some mistakes, and people will criticize you at times, but this is far better than settling for the status quo that isn't working. Richard was hired from a prominent university setting to head up a school in a suburban area within a short drive to a major city. He seemed to have all of the right credentials—diplomas from select colleges, experience in K-12 education, good references, and he was charming. What eventually led to his disappointment as leader and departure from the school was his inability to make decisions. He was frozen in place and feared making mistakes moving forward. At first, colleagues and parents in the community thought he was remarkably circumspect and unusually careful about drawing any hasty conclusions. However, within a short time, it became apparent that even the smallest decision, whether to cancel a soccer practice due to inclement weather or to plant flowers at the entrance of the school, created anxiety for him and frustration for those around him. With this personal predisposition, it would have been impossible for him to do what needed to be done to lead a school to excellence.

Jeffrey Pfeffer and Robert I. Sutton, authors of *The Knowing-Doing Gap, How Smart Companies Turn Knowledge into Action*, believe that fear such as the kind experienced by Richard can contribute to the knowing-doing gap. According to these business-school professors, fear can be multifaceted. The inaction may be caused by a variety of things: being a perfectionist, worrying about competition, and experiencing uncertainty as to how to proceed. If you are gearing up to lead change, which is a constant in schools, examine your own fear factor to be sure that it will not get in the way of success for the school.

Pfeffer and Sutton offer several other reasons why there might be a gap between knowing and doing. They believe that people and organizations often substitute mission for action and planning for action. Surely, your school needs a mission statement that is thoughtfully crafted and regularly visited to ensure that a common vision exists, but, despite the effort it takes to agree upon a mission statement for an institution, this is only the beginning. There has to a discernable link between the saying and the doing. See this as your job, even if you have inherited the mission statement. Organizations, including schools, often have or decide to develop a strategic plan, which is generally a good idea, however, once completed, the plan needs to be translated into a concrete action document. This should include a timeline for implementation and a point person responsible for each task. As principal, you will be overseeing this massive effort, making sure things get completed as designed, as well as doing your part in contributing to the whole. Without a well-thought-out action plan, a strategic plan that may have taken hundreds of man hours by various groups to assemble is literally worth nothing. Margo led her school community through the year-long strategic planning process with inclusivity, insight, and inspiration. An outside consultant was hired, focus groups were formed, themes were identified, drafts were written and rewritten, and in time a well-articulated strategic plan was approved by the board and attractively printed for the school community. Unfortunately, as happens in many cases, the principal and the planning team were exhausted by this complex and comprehensive task, so they never took the next critical step. Thus, the precious document sat on a shelf, looking good but contributing nothing to student engagement and achievement in that school.

This may be why certain organizational gurus dismiss strategic planning as archaic. They believe that doing is what matters. If you have an eager-beaver personality, this may sound like music to your ears—no wasted time spent on preliminaries—but beware of this logic. You need a plan to direct your doing. On the other hand, if you delight in amassing data, measuring opinions, designing systems, and putting it all together in one tidy package, realize that your efforts are only as good as the results they produce. Thinking has to lead to doing. As principal, take stock. Ask yourself the following questions: Do I know what needs to be done? Have I built a strong but not perfect platform for change? Are the goals clearly defined for everyone? Is getting the job done—not just writing about it and talking about it—the true measure of success? And am I able to respect the past without getting stuck there and help colleagues negotiate the stumbling blocks that will be in the way? Perseverance and focused concentration on your goals will steady your path.

Three

Cultivating Humility While
Charging Ahead

REALIZING PEOPLE MATTER

When you think of humility, what is the first image that pops into your head? Perhaps it is Mother Teresa, the elderly nun who tended the sick, the dying, and the poorest of the poor and believed, "It is easy to be proud, and harsh and selfish—so easy. But we have been created for better things." Or do your thoughts turn to someone like Mahatma Gandhi, the political and spiritual sage whose ideas and life of service influenced so many? Despite his modest words, "I claim to be no more than an average man with less than average abilities," he inspired other world leaders, including Desmond Tutu, Nelson Mandela, the Dalai Lama, and Martin Luther King Jr. These are heroes of humility who charged ahead, and while we may not aspire to their kind of sainthood, their approach to life can teach us a great deal. They didn't get bogged down with details and power. Without much fanfare, they just did what they were called to do. They channeled their time and energy and when many others criticized their work, they just dug in deeper. They spoke not of themselves but of a better world for others. They were not pretentious. Things didn't matter to them—people did.

As a principal, there is no better place to begin honoring people than by recognizing the past. Whenever you have the opportunity, speak charitably of your predecessors. Each leader leads with specific skills necessary for that time. As a new head, you may believe that you will take the school to the next level of excellence, which is admirable, but never forget those who did the heavy lifting before you. One founding school head had brilliant ideas about curriculum and instruction for young children. She selected materials that were attractive and unique and created structures for students that were innovative. Parents recognized immediately that this was an environment where learning was revered. What was not obvious was that the school had no systems in place for adults. The next head's job was to work on organizational issues of budgeting, communication, and space planning, never forgetting that the original school head made this possible.

If you come into a school that was clearly poorly run and there is no discernible leadership to recognize, focus on the job at hand, you never want to be the one bad-mouthing another person. As the new principal, your standards of behavior set the stage for the entire school community. Extend your appreciation beyond the former school heads and honor past or departing employees. When teachers or staff members retire or leave for personal reasons, give them a token gift with a handwritten note and have some communal celebration. Their contributions helped to make the school what it is. When they are gone, stay in touch periodically by having them substitute for a teacher or a staff member. They are valuable; they know the culture, the systems, and the people. Invite past employees to any school-wide celebration and send them any important news of the school. These people are your best ambassadors for the school. Use them.

Once you realize the value of people in an organization, choose to be compassionate. Some people are born with a tender heart; others have to work at it and make a conscious effort to care. It is a choice that is quietly but persistently present every moment of our day. You can ignore the hefty bags a colleague is carrying from the parking lot while you walk alongside chatting, with only a purse in hand. You can pretend to be busy when a staff member is looking for cables to jump-start the dead battery in his car. You can look the other way when another employee is clearly in distress, or you can choose to be compassionate.

When you do choose to care and show it, something happens inside of you. You feel needed, connected, and lighter, and for a brief moment, the world seems an extraordinary place. When you were giving, you were actually getting. Why should this matter at all in a school environment? Certainly, we'd like to think that in all communities and corporations people are choosing to be compassionate, but in schools it is essential. Children must have their basic needs met before they can begin to learn. When they know that someone really cares about them and shows it, they open up to endless possibilities. The principal, in a quiet and unassuming way, can initiate this chain of compassion on campus. By being the one to stop and help carry in the heavy bags for a colleague, by offering cables needed to jump-start the car, by noticing and responding to the employee in distress, the school head is showing the way and real teaching goes on. Actions always speak louder than words. A leader showing compassion consistently will communicate that this is important. When all of the adults on campus begin to show compassion to each other, it will become a natural way of interacting. This attitude and outreach will eventually trickle down to relationships with students; they will feel valued and want to learn.

In any organization, but especially in schools, people are the lifeblood. Everything else is secondary. As a principal you will have to bear this in mind with each decision you make and each exchange you have. Your mission is to be present in some way to the entire community. You will connect with groups: the PTA, the board, the superintendent's office, the staff, the leadership team, the student government, the academic committees, the building and ground crews, and special-project volunteers, however, remember that every group is made up of individuals, and this is where the real work of connecting is done. Begin by thinking about those individuals whom you see for extended periods each day. Consider your administrative assistant a partner. Don't even think in terms of principal versus staff member; you are allies. If you are to be all you can be as a principal, your administrative assistant will have to be at your side helping you each step of the way. Moreover, he or she will have duties not directly tied to your tasks, but how well these tasks are done will affect your position. Hand pick this person carefully, or, if you have inherited an administrative assistant, be clear from the beginning about what you expect in terms of performance and the relationship. If you have any doubts as to competence or loyalty, bail out earlier rather than later, and shop for someone whom you can see as a potential partner. You need this person's help to be a competent leader. Your partner will protect you from the wolves, be the schedule gatekeeper, and be a sounding board when you need an honest opinion. Recognize this vital relationship and never let your behavior indicate any superiority on your part.

You and your administrative assistant will spend most of your days working side by side, but at dusk, when the building is nearly empty, you will encounter another colleague. Get to know the person who cleans your office. There will be times when just the two of you will be in the building working. That you have this in common is enough for you to connect. In many communities recent immigrants are the people doing janitorial work, so a language barrier may be present. Don't let this stand in the way. Smiling and gesturing can often begin a relationship. Learn several phrases in his or her language. "Good evening," "How are you?" "Excuse me; let me get out of your way" are possible exchanges to master. Instant translation available on the Internet can help here. Introduce yourself and then greet this coworker daily by name and offer thanks for the work being done. Both of you are serving this community; both of you are part of something greater than yourselves.

If you truly realize how much people matter in a school, your leadership style should reflect this. At the very least, proceed mindfully. Imagine that every individual you come in contact with faces some challenges beyond what you can see. It could be a life-altering condition such as addiction, alienation, or any sort of serious physical or mental health illness, or it could be one of the mundane annoyances—a sassy teen, a leaky roof, or a fender bender—that threatens to do us all in. Bearing this in mind should alter the way you connect with people. Your touch should be gentle, your approach considerate. This sensitivity does not mean that you should write off your plans for school improvement, water down your standards, or even acknowledge the specifics. It just means being aware of other people and their angst. A leader who blindly goes about his business, sensing none of the pain around him, will walk alone with no followers pursuing the trail blazed.

WORKING ON ONE'S SELF

Contrary to some thinking, humility is not self-deprecation or spinelessness. It is, rather, accepting yourself as you are, with all of your strengths and weaknesses and believing that you are no better or no worse than any other human being. Leaders who cultivate humility begin to enjoy freedom that more prideful executives do not possess. Posturing and recounting past victories require enormous energy and time that could be put to better use. This freed up time and energy should then be spent on figuring out precisely how to grow as a leader. Swallowing pride is a good place to start. Admit what you don't know. Once you do this, work to find the answer or study to get up to speed. No one can be an expert in all things. People who don't know what they don't know are scary and dangerous. A school head worthy of the title needs to be reasonably self-aware and straightforward about any area of ignorance.

As a middle-aged principal who was new to the profession, Jared always played the tough guy role; he felt his military background gave him significant clout to do the job. Jared relied on bravado and his big voice, and he expected people to jump when they heard his orders. Unfortunately for him, this just didn't happen in civilian life. He had not earned his stripes in the world of schooling, and staff members and teachers knew it. His school faced enormous challenges that were often ignored due to his ignorance. A candid self-assessment would have made all the difference.

Along with admitting what you don't know, consider disclosing your vulnerability. People want strong leaders, but not inhuman ones. An honest touch of insecurity divulged here or a true spot of weakness displayed there makes others feel connected to you in some fashion. One veteran principal acknowledged being frightened by having to get a flu shot and frustrated by having to set up a new cell-phone system, thereby letting colleagues see the less-than-perfect side of her. This transparency brought out the best in others, inviting them to support someone else and bridge the gap between "I and thou."

As you work toward having a humble heart, cultivate awe. Babies are born curious, and young children spend their days functioning on a natural high, fascinated by everything around them. As we age, we lose this gift of first sight, and, if we are not mindful, our worlds may become monotonous. When we reengage our senses, several things happen. The world once again becomes a fascinating place. We feel more alive, and we begin to appreciate our place in the planet. Gradually, we grasp that we are playing a pretty minor role in the history of mankind. Holding an infant, watching the sunrise, baking bread, or listening to a live concert can stimulate our senses and help us recapture the wonders of our childhood. Principals who lose this sense of awe become pompous. As they succumb to the seduction of power, they become self-centered, unattractive leaders who turn people off. Wonder, on the other hand, leads to wisdom.

Education classes focus on content mastery and methods of instruction. Most of it is crammed with subject matter or is theoretical in nature. People with good memories who also had gifted professors can retain much of what is taught and are able to translate this to classroom instruction. Over time, however, the memory of how it *feels* to be a learner is lost. Moreover, many teachers and principals were achievers in school themselves; they loved school, so they have no innate sense of what real frustration is like or how hard learning can be for some students. Without this understanding, teachers and principals will not be able to reach all children. To appreciate the effort and focus it takes to learn something new, try learning to speak a foreign language, play an instrument or play golf...all challenging and humbling.

Sometimes growing humility in oneself requires what would be thought of as unexpected behaviors in a leader, such as refusing a principal's parking space. This radical act can go far in showing that you see yourself being on a team. The presumed perk of a privileged parking spot just sets you apart and can make you think you are special, when in truth you are just a cog in the wheel. A seasoned head was reminiscing about the time spent as a young administrator at various schools. When she was younger, she relished her parking spaces and felt she had earned them. Older and wiser as a school head at another school, she parked in the extended lot with the rest of the teachers and staff members. Each day trudging through the heat or rain or wind, she was reminded that she was not special. This promptly set the stage for the day's demeanor and decision-making. No number of exquisitely drafted memos to faculty and staff saying "We are a team" can compete with a principal parking next to you in the lot. Consider it.

Or, as you seek a more humble heart, be honest and surprise others by reversing a poorly made decision. You don't want to have to do this again and again, but when a decision clearly was a wrong one, admit it and move on. Inexperienced leaders believe that they must be infallible—an impossible goal to reach. Maybe you didn't have all of the facts to make an informed decision, or you listened to counsel and predicted outcomes that just didn't happen. Accept your fallibility. Some poor decisions are unavoidably public, like redesigning the carpool system that everyone said wouldn't work and they were right. Other decisions are more private, such as hiring someone whom you believed to be competent and then discovering that your judgment was faulty. Acknowledge the reality of your error and try to rectify it. In his first month of office, President Obama amazed everyone by saying, "I screwed up." This was not something the American people were used to hearing, and it was refreshing. With this honesty, the topic at hand was nearly forgotten due to the unexpected mea culpa.

Moving a step closer toward cultivating humility means being able to acknowledge the victor, practicing the words "You are right" and then saying them out loud when necessary. This sage advice comes from career coach Bruno Martinuzzi. Principals, like most people, sometimes can admit when they are wrong but often cannot take the next important step and say, "You are right." What an easy way to set the record straight, which often leads to more collaborative and creative teamwork. Cammy, a primary-school principal, was a pro. Her smile would melt the toughest opponent, and yet she could pack a punch when necessary. One of her secrets was her ability to listen, consider the information, and then without any ego getting in the way, say either, "No, your information is incorrect, so you understand, of course, why we did thus and so" or "Yes, I see your point. We did not understand the situation correctly. You are right to feel as you do." She was able to be a strong advocate for children, teachers, and parents by keeping an open mind and admitting when others were right.

Another simple practice for leaders aspiring to be humble is cleaning up your own messes. Seemingly small behaviors from leaders send large messages to followers. At the end of group meetings where brown-bag lunches were provided, a principal who often appeared to be in his own world would simply get up from the table, ignore his empty cup and sandwich wrappings, and walk away. He had grown so accustomed to other people cleaning up after him that he didn't even notice it. This attitude reflected a deeper and more serious character flaw in a leader. He was not in tune with his people and had no idea what they needed. His narcissistic behavior limited any real connection with colleagues and children, so his school was in peril, and he didn't even know it. An air of entitlement always extinguishes any esprit de corps. If only this failed principal had known the importance of cleaning up his own messes and helping others to do the same, he could have been a servant-leader with a following. Bear in mind that your messes will not be limited to lunch debris alone; they will include all kinds of thoughtless acts that you will unwittingly commit. When you clean up these messes, you will show faculty, staff, students, and parents the importance of accepting responsibility for one's own actions.

Being a school leader and beginning to grasp the importance of cultivating humility should affect not only your daily performance but also your thinking. Humility will inspire gratitude. You have an education, you have a job, and you get a paycheck. You live in America where you can worship as you please and speak your mind freely. The Constitution of the United States grants you incredible freedoms not enjoyed in many other parts of the world. It is important to remember this so that in your daily functioning as a school leader, you can resist the temptation to be petty, whiney, or narrow-minded. You are blessed. At a "Best Places to Work" awards ceremony one year, a school was selected to receive an award, and while there were other nonprofit organizations honored, this was the only school. Per instructions, each CEO was to come forward when the ranking was announced and tell the audience what this particular company did that made employees believe it was a great place to work. The table of ten from the school, selected randomly, began to giggle as they heard the competitors' perks: "homemade kolaches on Wednesdays, work at home in inclement weather, free beer on Friday," and so forth. The school group began to whisper back and forth in a lighthearted way, wondering what to say when it was their turn…"Complimentary parking; 'color day,' when we, like the students, all wear the same color; and free lice checks by the nurse." It may sound silly, but in a strange way it made the teachers and staff members realize that their world was vastly different from other organizations, and in a good way. They may not have gotten all the beer they could drink on Fridays, but they had the opportunity to change children's lives. What other organizations present could claim that honor!

Working your way up the leadership ladder or transferring to head another school is an opportune time to remind yourself to let go and move on. You may have been prom queen or valedictorian; however, that was then, and this is now. Appreciate past honors and welcome the new accolades that may come your way, but don't let them define you. Old football heroes or Phi Beta Kappa scholars who stay in that place seldom move on to create anything meaningful. Leaders of note are always looking up for the next mountain to climb, not looking down from their first mountaintop. Charlie was a case in point. He was hopelessly stuck in the past. His "Bula, Bula" fight song days at Yale were never far from his consciousness. Conversations often began with, "I remember one time at Yale when we…" Newcomers to the school were asked where they hailed from, and upon hearing the locale, Charlie would launch into his old refrain, "I bet you know my old friend Harvey from Pittsburgh or my best bud Dougie from Atlanta." Charlie never really grew up, and his fondest memories were of his college years. Faculty members found him quirky and let him go his own way while they did their own thing. Students sensed the disconnect and paid him no heed. Life was in limbo on this campus.

OPENING UP TO POSSIBLITIES

In military and corporate settings of the past, and perhaps still to this day, there are those who believe that a leader must be commanding and autonomous. Fortunately, Jim Collins, author of the bestseller *Good To Great: Why Some Companies Make the Leap…and Others Don't*, debunked this popular myth. Collins and his team of twenty-one people spent five years determining the variables that move a company from good to great. They wanted to know what great companies shared that distinguished them from comparison companies. Collins writes that he persisted in telling his researchers to "ignore the executives." But his research team kept pushing back, "No! There is something consistently unusual about them. We can't ignore them."

And they didn't, as the data demanded, finally at the end of the study discovering that "all good-to-great companies had level 5 leadership at the time of transition." For Collins, level 5 leadership translated to humility plus will, "a paradoxical mix of personal humility and professional will. They are ambitious first and foremost for the company, not themselves." He believed that these leaders were "fanatically driven, infected with an incurable need to produce sustained results" and displayed a "workman-like diligence—more plow horse than show horse." In order to charge ahead in pursuit of excellence for your school, you have to be diligent, yes, but you must not operate from your own small sphere of knowledge and experience. Rather you must open yourself up to possibilities beyond anything you may have ever imagined. This means a major shift in your perception from what you know to what you need to know. The solo flight that you imagined as a principal suddenly becomes a chartered group excursion.

In Zander and Zander's book *The Art of Possibility, Transforming Professional and Personal Life*, they state, "On the whole, resources are likely to come to you in greater abundance when you are generous and inclusive and engage people in your passion for life." A principal with an open-door policy who welcomes input and interesting ideas will be transformed, and the school, in turn, will thrive beyond anyone's wildest expectations. A parent in one school found out about a grant for solar energy and spearheaded this project, benefitting both academics and the budget with reduced-energy cost. A reading-resource teacher in a middle school read about the magic of literature circles and suggested that the school give them a try. With the head's blessing, this new system was instituted, and students responded enthusiastically. This approach especially helped reluctant readers. An athletic director, who was always thinking of student needs, requested that students be permitted to use the gym in the early mornings rather than just having them hang around the halls before class began. With the principal's OK and a schedule of volunteer adults to in place to supervise, this happened. Fitness improved, student relations across grade levels were more positive during pickup games, and focus in first period class was stronger… the wiggles were gone. If the principal had stuck to his agenda only, none of these things would have happened.

Benjamin Zander, conductor of the Boston Philharmonic, shared an interesting insight in *The Art of Possibility*: "I had been conducting for nearly twenty years when it suddenly dawned on me that the conductor of an orchestra does not make a sound. His picture may appear on the cover of the CD in various dramatic poses, but his true power derives from his ability to make other people powerful. I began to ask myself questions like 'What makes a group lively and engaged?' instead of 'How good am I?'" Humility always involves an otherness.

In your desire to cultivate openness, you have to welcome input from others. Be brave, and ask for feedback. Often principals believe in everyone else getting feedback, but are reluctant to ask for it for themselves. Admittedly, it does take a tough skin to hear what others have to say. Even if fifty comments are positive, most school heads who are closet achievers will pounce on the few negative comments listed and perseverate. They will ask themselves and close associates in hushed tones, "Am I am really aggressive? Do I truly interrupt and cut off other people's ideas? Am I too slow in responding to needs?" Listen and learn. The purpose of feedback is to hear what others are thinking. Once digested, continue the good things mentioned, without gloating, and then work on improving the deficiencies noted. There are various ways to get important feedback. Be sure that your supervisor conducts an annual performance review. If it is your first year at the school, it would be wise to ask for an assessment after three months. By that time you will be a bit more secure in the principal's chair but still green enough to want to hear about any bad habits and still eager enough to be assured that the path chosen, thus far, seems generally acceptable. At some point, ask your leadership team to fill out a feedback form anonymously. If you remain in a school for several years, it is a good practice to have an electronic survey sent to all constituents. These questions should address all areas of school life, including your leadership, but bear in mind that you are responsible for everything on campus, whether your name is attached to it or not. Once the survey results are gathered, a leader's role is to extend praise to others for positive things noted in the general assessment. With any comments related to your role, realize that whatever good you did, you didn't do alone, so extend gratitude. It is also your job to set about changes based on the data gathered. Meet with the employees in private or teams that are directly responsible, and set a game plan with them. In public, take the blame for anything that went wrong, even if it wasn't directly your fault. As the CEO, you cannot pass the buck.

One who "cultivates" pays attention to something in particular and is willing to till the soil until the seedlings blossom. This is what humility demands; it is slow developing but must be present while charging ahead in order to lead and have others want to follow. Even with extraordinary tenacity and patience, you are not in control. Do your best, work with conviction, and try to lead the community toward a clear vision of success for all students, but know that you do not hold all of the cards. Leaders who come to grips with this realization are able to sustain the necessary momentum of working toward goals without the paralyzing sense of guilt when things don't work out as planned. Sometimes this means just trying another approach, other times it means abandoning a project, and every once in a while it means resigning from the job.

Deanna and Carla were two experienced and able educators selected for leadership positions in a district. They were asked to convene focus groups, address key issues such as finance, and then craft numerous recommendations on how to improve education in their local schools. They were energized and enthusiastic about the duties handed to them. Regrettably, each report they turned in to their supervisor was dismissed, and other decisions were made without any dialogue or further discussion. Eventually, they both realized that their work was not valued, that the request for studies was a sham, and that they had no real input in decisions. With this insight, these two solid educators chose to move out of the district to positions where they could lead happier lives as professionals and affect meaningful change for students.

LEADING BY SERVING

Our egos that sustained us in childhood continue to want top billing as "show horses," but as we mature, our "me, me, me" demands should be replaced by "you, you, you" concentration. A true leader does not believe that he or she is the center of the universe. On the contrary, a leader must see the needs of others as paramount. Grasping this key point and then deciding to be humble is not a done deal. It takes work. Each notch in a leader's belt requires resisting that ego pull, which is always there waiting to be welcomed. To entertain the concept of a leader serving, a principal should become familiar with Robert K. Greenleaf, who first popularized this concept when he wrote an essay entitled "The Servant as Leader." While this idea had historical roots, his seminal piece published in 1970 has influenced and challenged countless theorists and practitioners since that time. This AT&T executive, now deceased, clearly shook up the corporate world when he wrote, "The servant-leader is a servant first."

While you are contemplating this notion, which may be an atypical approach in a principal preparation program, make your own coffee. Better yet, be like Priscilla, a successful principal, who arrived early each day to make the coffee for everyone else. She was a high-school principal in one of the top-ten suburban school systems in the country where excellence reigned. She supervised veteran educators who valued their placement in a top-tier school as well as young teachers from prestigious universities who were thought to be experts in their fields. Priscilla looked every bit the part of a professional, which probably served to elevate the office environment somewhat, but it was her service in making the morning coffee that set her apart from other leaders, which teachers and staff members noticed, making them want to follow her lead. By performing an everyday service such as making the coffee for colleagues, you are not only leading by serving but also modeling selflessness.

Extend your service outreach. Picking up trash around the school entrance or in the middle-school hallway sets an example that needs no words. If there is a school event, volunteer for the most unexpected and perhaps most unattractive post: cooking hot dogs in the canteen during the basketball tournament or cleaning up after the school fair. This modeling should be present but not blatant. You want your message to be delivered quietly and consistently so they get it. Marni, a young, fit middle-school principal, volunteered to sit in the dunking booth during field day and again and again was dunked into the water by her students who could aim a ball. Each time, she got out smiling.

Come up with something that you can be enthusiastic about. Rachel, an elementary-school head who was usually generous to a fault, declined the trustees' suggestion to dress up as a witch and climb up to the roof of the main school building on Halloween morning to welcome everyone. She felt she had to draw the leadership line somewhere. The ways in which you decide to model service to the school are not nearly as important as the fact that you are doing it. Elizabeth O'Connor, writer, teacher, counselor, and ecumenical leader, coined a phrase, "marks of love," which should aptly describe your service to the school. When you show your love for the place and for the people in it, others will see you as their leader and want to follow.

Realize that schools are part of the service industry. Although most public and private schools are nonprofit, seeking no direct financial benefit, they do have a product (education) to be delivered to customers (children, parents, and communities). Customers are choosy, as they should be, so if a school is not delivering a quality product, parents and children will go elsewhere if they can. Public and private schools need to fill their seats; budgets depend upon set numbers, and, furthermore, communities want to be proud of their schools. Good schools bring businesses and homes into an area and enrich the economy, which benefits everyone. A service mindset is essential for people who work in schools. The principal sets this tone by constantly modeling servant leadership and by not asking employees to do anything that he or she would not do. At one K-8 school, during the orientation for faculty and staff, as carpool assignments were being handed out, an irate teacher said, "I am not going to open car doors for these kids; I am not a servant." She had totally missed the point. Servant-leaders are exactly what teachers, staff members, and principals are. We are saying, through powerful actions, "At this school, this is how we live. We help each other."

Four

Bringing out the Best in Faculty and Staff

CREATING A CULTURE

The ultimate test for a leader is inspiring others to perform with passion at maximum proficiency. This sounds so simple but is difficult to achieve without knowing how to make it happen. Even in the military, with all of the rules and ranks, real leaders are able to enlist true followers because of who they are and how they lead, not merely because of what is demanded. In schools, where leadership changes frequently, concern and confusion can reign. Even if a school is not run well, there is some security for the community in knowing the way the game is played. Any change is threatening. Anything different is disorienting and at first unwelcome.

Your job as a new school head is to instill confidence without being arrogant and to share a vision for a brighter future without dismissing the past. A steadfast sensitivity to others and a judicious management of the schedule of changes will be your best allies. Your potential followers, the faculty and staff, may respond albeit grudgingly to your new edicts—arrive at school on time, and lock your classroom and office doors when not in use—when the expectations are clear and measurable. More intangible expectations—show respect to everyone and make student learning a priority—are difficult to judge and require not just rules but also individual buy-in. This takes time and work on your part. Teachers and staff members must connect directly with you and believe in your dream or they will revert to old behaviors behind closed doors.

Creating a new culture is perhaps the most difficult job for a principal, yet it is at the center of any change initiative. You do this by words, of course, but mostly by actions. If you are purposeful and genuine, the shift will be noticeable. Begin with the basics. Get in the habit of saying "please" and "thank you," even if you are asking people to do things that are part of their jobs. When you say these words and really mean them, a bond is forged, but don't fake this. Everyone can smell a phony, which is worse than no thanks at all.

Even though you are itching to get on with projects, pace yourself. One of your operational goals for this new culture is to generate a calm atmosphere. Multitasking mad men may look productive, but they also create a milieu that is frenetic and contagious that can result in testy workers who are prone to mistakes. Most experienced principals can recall times during their tenure when a fever pitch was necessary to finish a project requiring all hands on deck, but this cannot be the norm if you want quality work delivered by loyal, long-term employees.

Consider the individuals who will play a part in this new culture. Bill Gates believes, "As we look ahead to the next century, leaders will be those who empowered others." This view should encourage you to hold the reins of your leadership team loosely. You have inherited or hired people with talent and experience. Use their gifts and give them space and time to try their hands at leadership within their area of responsibility. Let them know that you value innovation that is backed up with solid research and is executed thoughtfully. Their attempts will not be successful 100 percent of the time, and that is OK. They need to feel supported in their search for excellence and know that unless an egregious error surfaces or they prove to be generally incompetent, you will be behind them. Insecure horsemen who grasp the reins too tightly create tension and choke natural talent. Relax and remember the harness is still in your hands. Don't follow Monica's example. She was an elementary-school administrator who, despite her good cheer and enviable social skills, was never able to let go of the smallest of details, and her habit of constantly looking over everyone's shoulder made the leadership team feel infuriated and impotent. Most found greener pastures.

Look beyond the leadership team in building a new culture. Involve staff members. Teachers rule in the classrooms, but staff members run everything else and enable teachers to teach. There is a tendency for some principals to establish a pecking order in schools. Back-to-school orientation is for faculty only, risk-management discussions occur among the administrative team in isolation, and behavior in the cafeteria or bus procedures are staff problems to solve. Don't get caught in this narrow way of looking at people. Whenever possible, have representatives from various parts of the school community gather to discuss what is working and what is not. At times, someone not particularly close to an issue will ask the critical questions and offer the most innovative solutions.

Jack Welch, leadership expert and legendary CEO at General Electric, states in *25 Lessons for Leaders*, "Involve everyone and get great ideas from everywhere. New ideas are the lifeblood of an organization." Don't let your outreach stop there. Widen your circle. Include the peripheral personnel in your leadership scope. Lucy, a tiny dynamo of a school head who could have run IBM single-handedly, invited the bus drivers for a breakfast meeting in her office once a month. This let them know they were important in her eyes and helped sort out little issues before they became big problem, which was brilliant—most principals soon find out that many disciplinary matters, everything from unwelcome sex education to bullying, happen on the bus ride to and from school.

Treat your substitutes with TLC, even if you don't work with them directly; know that you cannot operate the school without them. One principal always sent her squad of regular subs a Valentine thank-you to let them know they were appreciated. Meet with the coaches or other organized youth leaders who work on your campus. They need to know school standards, school policies, and your personal expectations concerning safety, discipline, parent communication, and school communication. Don't assume that because they work in a school, they understand the culture of the campus or the inherent values in place.

Your ways of dealing with people and problems will significantly shape the culture, however, in your eagerness to be inclusive and empower others, don't expect that all will go swimmingly. Address mistakes made. We are all human and prone to missteps, but when mistakes do happen, don't sweep them under the carpet. Talk to the person who used poor judgment or acted impetuously, and together try to figure out how this could be avoided in the future. Bear no grudge, but also be clear that this cannot be repeated. If the situation is serious enough, write an incident report that you both sign, just in case you may have to use this as part of an improvement plan or a dismissal procedure. As a principal, you will have to use your judgment as to which way to proceed based on the seriousness of the offense, school and district policies, the contrition of the offender, and his or her past record of behavior. In some instances where a law is broken, there is injury, or potential damage to the school exists, a principal will have to move swiftly and surgically. Faculty and staff handbooks should spell out expected behavior codes and list reasons for immediate dismissal. Each employee should sign this handbook signaling understanding and compliance prior to employment.

Early on in a principalship, it is a smart move to take a seminar on hiring and firing within the law. School systems do provide guidance, but the individual principal needs to know the pitfalls to avoid. Barbara, a dignified public elementary-school principal who was a picture of composure at all times, could never bring herself to discuss a problem she was aware of with an employee, so she quietly seethed inside and nothing changed. Jack, on the other hand, a bearded free spirit who was a head of an alternative private high school where everyone, including students, called each other by first names, complained about everything after the fact, but he had no policies to enforce. Both of these school heads would have been more effective leaders if they had known the importance of addressing missteps when they occurred and had policies in place clearly defining rules and procedures.

While you are doing your best to address mistakes, make every attempt to judge actions, not people. Lots of behavioral issues will find their way to your desk, and you will have to dole out some consequences that are not pleasant. The most severe issues, such as expelling a student or firing an employee, are painful for everyone. Try to separate the act from the person. The teacher who yells needs professional support for anger management and possibly counseling for a change of career. The student who has failed three core subjects needs an educational battery of tests to find out why, so he has a chance to be successful in another educational setting. As the school leader, you have a critical role to play in being present for those who have failed in some way. You have to help them understand that there are logical consequences for their behavior but that you care about them and will help them move forward. You must personally believe that change is possible for most people and accept that you have a part to play in this transformation. In time, with this approach, you will see people turn their lives around. Often these are the sweetest successes in a school head's career.

What you value and how you proceed will contribute enormously to the new culture you are creating. Be confident enough to take calculated risks. Principals who constantly play it safe in hiring, scheduling, or curriculum development rarely improve student involvement and achievement. Roberto, the principal in a low-income Southwest school, decided to capitalize on his talented music teacher and began a strings program for elementary students. Many obstacles had to be overcome, from instrument rentals to parent buy-in, but it worked! Rough-and-tumble little boys soon began to play violins, violas, cellos, and basses, and as their musical skills grew, their self-esteem blossomed and their math scores improved. At a suburban private school, Scott hired a recently retired army officer with advanced math degrees to teach math to middle-school students. This gentleman had no teaching credentials, and while he had the academic background and experience leading a battalion, he had never worked in a school. The first day of class, this former military-officer-turned-novice-teacher filled an entire whiteboard with equations, geometric shapes and proofs, and lengthy algorithm solutions. Unfortunately, he didn't realize he was using a permanent marker. This was his only acclimation snafu. After this initial humiliation, he went on to become a gifted math teacher, and achievement scores zoomed.

CONNECTING WITH EMPLOYEES

If you want to lead, you must know something about those who are to follow. Depending upon the size of your school, your approach will vary; however, your goal should be to know something about each employee beyond his or her position. Just keeping your eyes and ears open will help in this regard. See who parks a truck next to yours in the school lot, check out the pet photos on desks, and notice the tennis racquet in the corner of an office. These are all clues to the person. With this approach, you will gradually begin to know your colleagues as individuals. While walking in to school, say to the person strolling along with you, "How was your week-end…did you do anything fun?" Strike up a conversation with someone in the lunch line: "Say, do you ever grill hamburgers at home?" Remember these chats so you can check in later with this person and resume some sort of casual relationship. Connecting with a community is not instantaneous. It happens slowly and meaningfully if the leader is conscientious about reaching out to others. If you are secretly shy, that is OK. Asking questions is a good way to open a conversation and to let people know that you care. A school is better served by a somewhat self-effacing leader than by a principal who is self-centered and oblivious to those around him.

Zero in on new teachers and staff members. As principal, how you engage with these new employees early on makes a real difference in their performance going forward. Don't just hire and then breathe a sigh of relief that you found that physics teacher or facilities director and forget about them. They need you, not just others, to tell them what is expected on this campus and to show them examples of the culture or how things are done around here. Whether they are brand-new or experienced teachers coming from another school, they cannot immediately grasp the academic standards you have set or the particular style of instruction your school favors. If staff members are coming from the corporate world or even another nonprofit organization, working in an academic setting will be vastly different; they need you to help them acclimate quickly so they can get down to business.

Your school size will determine how you reach out personally to these new hires. In a large school, you may have an initial meeting with them and then follow up later. Just don't let the size of the school deter you from making these important connections. Even though you may have two hundred employees, the new hires want to know you and what you think. If you miss this golden opportunity, they may connect with someone else—perhaps the curmudgeon that is always eager to share what is wrong with the school. In a smaller school, without extra administrative help, the task is all yours, which should be a pleasure. New hires are usually eager to please.

Ideally, it is a good idea to invite all new employees to a breakfast or lunch meeting during orientation week. You provide the food to make it special, which it is. This is a meeting just between you and them. It is not a time to find out about health insurance or parking permits. It is a time for them to bond with each other and to feel welcome and safe in your presence. Let them know how grateful you are that they are now in the school family and that their talents will help students thrive. If the group is not too large, have each person tell something about him or herself that is not part of their résumé. You can begin by relaxing everyone and mentioning that you have taken tap-dance lessons or love to play charades. They will get the idea and follow suit. This is the first step in getting to know new colleagues. Then tell them that this group is their survival team and that even if they have a mentor, everyone here is in the same boat and is to be a lifeline to each other. Encourage them to seek each other out at faculty/staff meetings or in the cafeteria. Particularly if a young person has come from another city for a job, this informal network of new employees is essential for success in a school. Have another gathering for new employees a month later, same format, you and them alone, and let them check in with each other, sharing challenges and victories. You can taper these meetings off during the year, but schedule them every few months or so as it seems worthwhile.

All new employees should have an evaluation after three months. You want to praise things well done and bring up needed changes. Principals should ask new teachers for a suggested time during the first six weeks that they may come into the classroom to observe. Then schedule a time with the teacher to give feedback in an informal way. This is not a written evaluation that goes in their personnel file but a snapshot view of what has been seen. Be specific. Mention things that you noticed that were great: "Jane, your book corner is so creative and inviting to second graders." and things that need changing: "Stuart, when you give homework assignments to middle-school students, it cannot just be verbal instructions. Hand out directions or print on the board so students can get the information by several senses." Obviously, to do this well, you must be observant and take notes of what you have seen. Honesty blended with kindness helps people grow.

How can a relationship thrive if you are operating in separate spheres all the time? Bridging the gap is up to you. Attend faculty meetings occasionally, even if you are not leading them. The key word to note is *occasionally*. Of course, you cannot attend all school meetings, but you cannot bail out altogether and become disengaged. If you make it a habit to drop into meetings occasionally, the teachers or staff members will nod to each other, knowingly, "Ah, it's business as usual; he cares what is going on here." A semiannual appearance, on the other hand, panics everyone and they wonder, "What is wrong? What did we do? Why is she here?" You must connect with the people doing the real work of educating. Be deliberate; have your administrative assistant insert all meetings into your calendar, and then highlight those you plan to attend. Don't let your relationships be all business, either. Make it a point to attend the periodic faculty and staff party or baby shower. This shows your human side and gives you an opportunity to laugh and spend some social time with your coworkers. Fight the urge to say, even to yourself, that you are too busy to attend. Everyone is busy. As you get to know your colleagues better and better, whenever you can, share the limelight. Your job as principal is to grow adults as well as students. At school meetings or public arenas, introduce a teacher or the athletic director, praise them for something tangible, and give them a chance to speak briefly. This approach shows your teamwork to the audience and demonstrates to your colleagues the confidence you place in them. With this heartfelt approach, more good things will follow.

Your employees will look to you for all sorts of reassurance. Uppermost in their minds is a concern for fairness. Be sensitive to equity, but also understand its complexity. Most rules apply to everyone, those being the important policies for safety, security, ethics, and integrity. Then there are rules that may have exceptions. School may begin at 7:30 a.m. for all faculty and staff, but your athletic director may be permitted to arrive later if he does not have an early-morning class because the basketball game kept him at school until 10:30 p.m. The handicapped parking places may be reserved for drivers with handicapped plates or stickers, but you as principal may make an exception and let the seven-months-pregnant teacher park there so she does not have to walk to the far faculty lot loaded down with a heavy laptop and a tote full of papers to correct. Issues of equity can be a hornet's nest on campus if employees are not assured that fairness is always in the mind of the school leader. Principals who strive to be equitable and hold everyone on campus (students, faculty, staff, trustees, visitors) to the same standards can help the community grasp that equity does not mean equality.

Besides equity matters, faculty and staff members will be most interested in getting you on their side for anything that affects them. Guard against taking sides in disputes. Various contingents will be at your door daily lobbying for your vote. After all, you are the chief decision-maker in their minds. The science department will want the gym for a science fair, bumping Friday's physical-education classes. The middle school will want to change the lunch period schedule, messing up the lower school's recess. The athletic department will want a pep rally last period, meaning the tests planned will have to be rescheduled. It is deadly to jump in prematurely. You want to be sure that the facts are aired and possible solutions are discussed. The best scenario is to have the stakeholders in the same room, and let them problem solve together to develop a win-win situation. Your role is best played by being the facilitator. When troubles from the outside storm against the schoolhouse door, you want to be present for your employees and stand behind them. Teachers and staff members in a school often take enormous flak for things beyond their control: a delayed school opening, a playground accident, or a cyberbullying incident. Find out all you can about the situation, be willing to be part of a solution if at all possible, and support your employees.

COMMUNICATING WITH FACULTY AND STAFF MEMBERS

Your employees need to hear from you so they can translate your ideas about teaching, learning, and creating a culture of excellence into specific practices. Help your faculty members understand the most important thing about teaching: showing students that you like them, respect them, and want to help them learn. Teachers need to know the content of their specialty and the best ways to teach their subject, but that alone won't ensure success. Becca was a youthful second-grade teacher with honey-blond hair and a broad smile. She wore colorful flowered blouses in the fall and textured snowflake sweaters in the winter. The seven-year-old boys in her class all fell in love with her. The girls wanted to dress like her and be like her…all except one. Norma was not like the rest. Her classmates shunned her for her annoying habits, and her teacher could not hide her distaste either. By the end of the first semester, it was a stalemate. Becca could not stand Norma, and as a result, Norma's behavior got worse and worse. Becca asked the principal to transfer the child to another class. The principal, in turn, asked Becca to identify one positive thing about Norma. Finally, after some time, Becca said, "She is a great speller." This was the turning point for the teacher, the child, and the class. Norma's natural gift of spelling helped ease her slowly into the group with the structured support of the teacher and the gentle but firm hand-holding of the principal. You will face this situation again and again at all grade levels of schooling. You must teach teachers this important lesson so they can truly teach every student.

Encourage teachers to tell parents good news when it is warranted. Usually when teachers call or send e-mails, "José has missed five assignments in math" or "Miranda has gotten into another fight on the playground," parents feel scared or depressed. Emotionally, this may trigger a memory of their own schooling and perhaps of a time when things did not go well for them, either. The past, present, and future often collide in parenting, and school-related matters somehow weigh heavily. Certainly teachers need to stay in contact with parents, but when they do, most of the time it is bad news. Mike, who had a lengthy career teaching math, English, and science in public and private schools, had a secret weapon for encouraging engagement and academic achievement. He called parents when their child had made an A on a particularly difficult test or when their child had worked really hard and brought a D average up to a B. This brought smiles and fueled further success. To help you stay connected, ask your faculty and staff to keep you informed of any matter that is noteworthy. You need to know the successes so you can publicize them and applaud the individual students before it is published in the school news. You need to know that a school-board member's son failed several subjects and thus is not eligible for football so you can prepare an offense before the phone call comes in. Tell your teachers that you do not like surprises, and then treat the teachers in a similar manner.

View feedback for administrators, staff members, and teachers as a gift. It takes time to observe, prepare, and discuss performance, but it dignifies the work being done and enhances professional development. Without faithfully adhering to this system, your meetings with individuals become routine calendar agenda items or occasional "caught in the act" comments given in passing such as: "Charles, I loved seeing you stop to talk to that child who appeared sad" or "Maria, please don't use sarcasm with your middle-school students; it is not appropriate." A performance evaluation appointment set aside for everyone from dean to receptionist says, "You are worthy of focus." This is an opportunity to discuss professional and personal goals and to examine what has gone well and what has not gone as well. The supervisor and employee should be expected to come prepared with notes to discuss these things. Details should be discussed, but the conversation should ideally go from the practical to the more abstract. As employees remain in a school, their performance evaluations should become records of their professional and personal growth under the guidance of a wise and caring supervisor. Each feedback session should set the stage for the next rung on the ladder of success as an educator or staff member.

CARING ABOUT COLLEAGUES

Your competence as a school leader is most evident in the ways that you show respect and care for your teachers and staff members. If you want them to be their best selves, you must be at their sides, supporting them professionally and personally. Sometimes this requires Herculean strength and stamina, and at other times, as natural leaders intuit, little things make all the difference. When Supreme Court Justice Elena Kagan became dean of Harvard Law School in 2003 and faced some incredible challenges, she said, "When I got here I looked around for little things I could do that don't cost much money, don't cost much time, that you don't have to have a faculty meeting to do. As it turns out…you can buy more student happiness per dollar by giving people free coffee than anything else I've discovered" (*Boston Sunday Globe*, October 19, 2008). She knew that little things send big messages.

You don't have to be a legal scholar in a prestigious setting to grasp this. Jeff, a homeless veteran who worked as a day laborer, got it too. Despite his on again, off again minimum-wage jobs, he had a long-term goal: to get a master's degree so he could "be the man." Why? So he could treat his workers well. He had experienced the ugliness of many bosses and believed that if he were in charge and had the opportunity to treat his workers with respect and care, they would outperform any team.

Besides providing coffee, to show you care, feed your people. Remember Maslow's "Hierarchy of Needs" from your psych classes? Food is one of the most primitive needs at the bottom of the pyramid. People who work in schools do not have the luxury of going off campus for lunch as many other professionals do, and for whatever reason, teachers work up longshoremen appetites. You would never imagine that Victoria had such an appetite. She weighed less than a hundred pounds and dressed in various dramatic combinations of black, which made her look even skinnier. Yet after elegantly conducting a complicated Orff piece or directing a recorder concert, she would head to the school cafeteria during lunch and outeat most coaches. She is just one of many teachers who need fuel to function well, so for faculty meetings, always include food if you can. If their stomachs are rumbling and they are feeling grouchy, you will lose them. Because it's important, even if funds are scarce for this sort of thing, you have to be creative in making it happen. Use some of your own discretionary principal monies, ask departments to chip in occasionally to sponsor a faculty meeting, have parents bring in snacks, solicit neighborhood restaurants for food samples, and, if all else fails, have teacher teams bring in snacks on a rotating basis. Bonding over chips and dip is a good way to begin a meeting and get important things accomplished.

As a school head who shows respect and care, assume that your employees will face physical challenges. In any group, you must expect that there will be illnesses and accidents. Fortunately, the bulk of those experienced by your faculty and staff will be transitory and minor. There will be the usual flu and respiratory bugs that almost everyone will battle in a building filled with children. Sharing symptoms and suggesting remedies will become the topic of discussion during a siege of aches and coughs on campus. There also will be emergency appendectomies, bunion surgeries, and skiing accidents to face. You will somehow muddle through these inconveniences together with substitutes filling in gaps and everyone lending a hand. More serious illnesses or accidents, however, will test your cohesiveness as a community. Simon was the catalyst for growth in one school community. He moved to the United States from Oxford, England, where he had spent years teaching middle-school students. Delighted to be in America and have the opportunity to teach adolescents in a different environment, Simon embraced everything with gusto. He whizzed through the American novels to be studied in class, wolfed down the corn dogs served for lunch in the cafeteria, and won the hearts of the seventh graders when he acted out the beheading of Anne Boleyn in English class. Surrounded by teachers, staff members, and students from the States, Simon had no choice. He just had to be who he was, an educated Brit with a twinkle in his eye, a charming English accent, and a sense of drama in his teaching. Stateside, he joined a soccer team and enjoyed the competition and the camaraderie, but by January of his first year, Simon was facing a facing a dire medical condition—melanoma on his leg. Chemotherapy was begun in earnest; however, it took its toll on this man in his prime. He needed days off for therapy and more days off to recuperate. By spring, it was clear that the cancer was advancing rapidly. Simon had to make some serious decisions, which he did with dignity and resolve. He decided to return home to England where he knew he would die. His American colleagues were astonishing. They had known him for less than a year, yet they rallied in ways not imagined. On their own, they passed a hat and sent him off with a full purse. They gave him farewell messages of hope and love. Simon came in and out of their lives so quickly, but he was one of them, and they responded with collective goodness. Grave illnesses or serious incidents may come into your community at some point. Your job is to have sown the seed of compassion on campus so that your employees will act from their hearts.

In addition to physical challenges that may affect your professional community, expect to deal with the emotional upheavals and more serious mental health issues of your employees. The National Institute of Mental Health (NIMH) estimates that one out of four adults "suffers from a diagnosable mental disturbance in a given year." This includes depression, anxiety, phobias, and bipolar disorders. Sometimes emotional meltdowns by teachers or staff members are to be expected and usually are short lived. A five-year-old may have had more than his share of troublemaking in the morning, pushing a kindergarten teacher's patience to the limit. An angry parent may have called an algebra teacher three times before class even began to challenge a child's test grade, making the teacher feel defensive and ready to fantasize about an alternative career! These types of meltdowns in teachers can be handled by collegial support or wise counseling of an administrator.

Other emotional upheavals are often the result of some event, external to the school—the breakup of a long-term relationship, the death of a loved one, or the care of a handicapped or critically ill child. In situations such as these, where the situation is affecting an employee's functioning and well-being, you as the school head must become involved. The support the employee needs will vary according to the situation, but usually time and a loving touch will help heal these wounds.

Given the NIMH estimates, know that more serious mental illnesses also will affect your faculty and staff. Schools can be stressful places, so often serious mental health issues surface in the workplace. Age and gender are no predictors. Catherine was a jovial woman who spent years enriching the lives of preschool children. She loved her work, and everyone loved her. One day, the four-year-olds in her class were being their usual creative and contrary selves, and instead of coping as she always did, Catherine just snapped. She did no real harm but went to the piano, turned her back on the children, and began singing in a loud voice to drown out the chaos surrounding her. Outside intervention was necessary. Bob was an eager young man who could not wait to become a teacher. He excelled in his university's teaching program and secured a position in a good school. Each morning he was one of the first to arrive and had his plans for the day finely detailed. During the first few weeks, the high-school students tested him a bit in class, which he just chalked up to his youthful appearance. All seemed to be going fairly well for this novice teacher until back to school night. The principal introduced the faculty and staff, and then the teachers were free to go to their rooms to await the parents, while the principal made a few general remarks about the program. Within this short time, Bob had a major panic attack. He hid in the closet of his classroom, unable to face the parents. It would have been difficult for a principal to have predicted this in such a promising young professional.

Probably the most challenging aspect of mental illness is that there are no casts or crutches that say, "Hey, pay attention; I am hurting." Your task is formidable. You have to protect the privacy of the employee suffering from a mental health condition, while trying to determine how serious it is and if the person can continue working. It may be that the condition has not been diagnosed, so you have to help the employee recognize the signs that may require medical attention. In addition to supporting school employees, your job is to protect the children and see that they are being educated. You need wisdom to serve everyone in these situations.

Show care for your employees by creating a wellness program in your school. Substitutes are necessary naturally, but regardless of their skills, they cannot replace the regular teacher in the classroom. In most schools, teachers are given one day a month for personal use, illness, or family demands. As principal, you want to keep teachers in the classroom as much as possible. New teachers are often the ones who miss the most school days until they become immune to the germs that are part of school environments. These teachers need your understanding of time off of work for illness.

To help fight obesity, high blood pressure, fatigue, depression, eating disorders, and more, think of ways that you can support your employees. Some schools offer free flu shots, some have weight clubs where members contribute nominal dues, weigh in weekly, and monthly give the person who lost the most weight the monies collected. Some have casual faculty and staff soccer or basketball teams to help reduce pounds and relieve stress. Don't let the lack of money destroy your dreams. At one school in a low-income neighborhood, Daryl, a wise and industrious principal, got his corporate sponsors to chip in some monies to purchase a few secondhand exercise machines to place in the small faculty room, along with a sofa, refrigerator, and microwave. Follow his lead, and work on outfitting a space for your employees as an indication of your respect and care. Regardless of the equipment donated, be sure that your school has a space for employees to go where no students (including children of employees) or parents are ever allowed. This will enable teachers and staff members to recharge, which they need to do to function well and serve students. As part of your professional development programs, occasionally include a health feature such as a nutrition expert, a yoga instructor, or a psychologist.

CHANGING MINDS AND HEARTS

In any real change at a school, either a significant culture redefinition or a sweeping curriculum conversion, your presence as principal is essential. Depending upon the size of your school and your budget, you may be fortunate enough to have a curriculum specialist or administrative support in assistant principals or division heads, but if you plan to institute any real change, everyone in the community needs to see you at the decision table armed with knowledge, commitment, and enthusiasm. You may have experts assisting you in technology, reading, writing, and mathematics, but don't rely on their experience and know-how to sell any change. Personally, you have to have sharpened your skills in targeted areas, become convinced of the needed change, and have explored the likelihood of success using a new approach in order to be able to communicate to teachers or staff members why change is necessary. Once decisions are made, be clear that the direction is not negotiable, while suggestions are always welcome for the execution.

When you have delivered the basic change message, begin to unroll the implementation process. Bear in mind that you have two different change challenges in employees: groups and individuals. The accounting department as a whole may welcome the newly recommended software program, but the bookkeeper who loves her current system may balk at the proposal and publicly make waves about the cost of the new program. Or the reading-resource teacher may be solidly behind a new reading series that emphasizes fluency and comprehension as much as decoding, while the primary teachers drag their feet at the thought of switching texts and daily instruction protocols. Your job is to address both the groups and the individuals who are wrestling with the change process, letting them know that you have utmost faith in their ability to do what is best for the children and the school. Also assure those who will be affected by any significant change that you will provide educational support as needed. Then, be true to your word on this. Many educational reforms have failed for lack of continuous professional development for new programs. Once the decision has been made to change some basic part of a school program, fight for the monies needed to help employees manage this new direction.

Schools usually have minimum hours required for professional development. Consider this just the baseline for maintaining talent. Any change initiative demands new attitudes and skills. You want everyone on the campus, including yourself, to be working on ways to improve performance, which will affect students and their learning. Don't limit this expectation to teachers alone. Staff members such as the nurse, librarian, receptionist, cafeteria workers, and others should be part of this educational push. How they do their jobs can directly and indirectly influence educational outcomes. Look at the number of advanced degrees on your faculty, and see how you can help individual teachers who are considering going back to school. Sometimes what teachers need most is encouragement. Talk to them about their dreams, support them while they take that first step to apply, fill out recommendation forms as requested, and then once they are enrolled, periodically check in to see how they are faring. As a school leader, you must see your role as growing adults as well as children. Find ways to keep growing yourself, which will not only increase your knowledge base but also inspire others. As management guru Stephen Covey says, "Keep sharpening your saw." Buildings, books, and technology all contribute to education, but people make the difference in student achievement, so invest in people.

Real change takes time to take root in a school. Be organized in your change process, set up a calendar to manage success, get key folks on board early, recognize the importance of teacher-to-teacher or staff-to-staff support in the acclimation process, and involve everyone in the transformation.

Understand that individuals and groups will vary in their adaptation, and accept that some people will not be able to manage change at all. They will be stuck in a professional place that includes only Saxon Math or QuickBooks Software. In cases where after a suitable transition time flexibility and an open mind still don't exist, you need to restate the new direction and encourage the employee to find other organizations that may be a better match. If this fails, take the necessary steps toward reassignment or dismissal. You don't want anyone working for the school that is not actively supportive of its philosophy and programs. When the vision is shared, the expectations are clear and employees believe they are valued and are making a difference in the lives of students and families, they will outperform people in a school community that is led by a principal who operates without intentionality.

Five

Keeping Centered in a Chaotic World

ANTICIPATING HURDLES

An earnest and energetic school head has a clearly defined vision for student success, a thoughtfully considered change plan for the community, and a well-crafted calendar in hand to drive the whole process. Everything seems promising and predictable. The principal heaves a sigh of relief that the heavy lifting is done. This state of nirvana is fleeting, however. Gradually, the leader discovers that the best-laid plans are only the beginning of an arduous journey.

The first indicators of trouble may surface within the school. Employees may squabble among themselves over seemingly mundane matters—who didn't show up for carpool duty, who left the faculty and staff room a mess, and who ignored the weekly testing schedule. Particular institutional stressors may contribute to turmoil in a school—why is the new grading software so difficult to use, why are our budgets frozen for the rest of the year, and why do teachers and staff members have to park in the faraway lots for graduation? External issues can also affect a school significantly. Weather related challenges—excruciating heat or cold, an ice storm, or a tornado warning—may add to the mix of pandemonium and put everyone on edge. Catastrophic events—a rape or assault on campus, an intruder with a weapon in the schoolyard, a highly contagious and dangerous disease in the community, and a fire or flood that could destroy everything in its path immediately halt any well-thought-out steps toward school improvement. Consider the attacks of 9/11, and contemplate the fragility of our world.

Tim never imagined how a hurricane could wreak havoc on a school and on his life. He moved to New Orleans to head a school in a town known for laid-back residents who partied with gusto and enjoyed their rich heritage of many cultures. Hurricane Katrina in 2005, however, brought Tim and everyone else up short, and the fun soon turned to months of worry about lives, property, and livelihood. Only when it was determined that students, families, faculty, and staff were out of harm's way and sheltered in temporary housing was the notion of schooling even considered. Then the practical problems surfaced. How extensive was the damage to the school buildings? Would insurance cover the costs? Was it possible to get to the area to make repairs, and were there workmen available? When would utilities be restored? Would school families return to the area or relocate? Were the school records destroyed? Which faculty and staff members would leave? How would grading and promotions be determined? What would happen to college applications? Could bills be paid and salaries honored? How long would reconstruction take, and how would the students be schooled in the unknown interim?

Tim was an educator with twenty-five years of experience under his belt and yet he too was stretched to the limit. Nevertheless, he pressed forward, focusing on the needs of the school, not on the damages to his own living space nearby. It was his calm, collaborative leadership that carried the school through the endless nightmare. By communicating through the power of the Internet, displaying a heartfelt empathy for everyone affected by the disaster, and by employing a judicious use of humor, Tim and his leadership team were able to bring this school community back to life, although not without serious struggles. Not all hurdles are as devastating as the hurdles school principals in New Orleans had to face with Hurricane Katrina, but be assured they are there. As a school head, forge ahead with your vision and your agenda for engaging and educating all children in your school, being aware at the same time that things may come out of the blue, creating chaos in your world. You don't want to be known as a Chicken Little who constantly bemoans, "The sky is falling," and you don't want to be so naïve as to believe that what you plan will come to pass without any glitches. Find the balance.

BECOMING SELF-AWARE

Begin by trying to find out the source of your strength. Dig deep to find that source of wisdom that nourishes your truest self. It may be an organized religion that centers you. Nature may be your inspiration; you may find peace by walking in the woods or sitting by water. You may find meaning in your life by reading myths, biographies, or poems. You may find strength in long-held family values and traditions. Regardless of what source deepens your sense of who you are, honor it, and return again and again for renewal. Otto Scharmer writes in *Theory U,* "We can look at a leader's work from three different angles. First we can look at what leaders do. Tons of books have been written from that point of view. Second, we can look at the *how,* the processes leaders use. That's the perspective we've used in management and leadership research over the past fifteen or twenty years. We have analyzed all aspects and functional areas of managers' and leaders' work from the process point of view. Numerous useful insights have resulted from that line of work. Yet we have never systematically looked at the leaders' work from the third, or blank canvas perspective. The question we have left unasked is 'What sources are leaders actually operating from?' I first began noticing this blind spot when talking with the late CEO of Hanover Insurance, Bill O'Brien. He told me that his greatest insight after years of conducting organizational-learning projects and facilitating corporate change is that the success of an intervention depends on the *interior condition* of the intervener. That observation struck a chord. Bill helped me understand that what counts is not only *what* leaders do and *how* they do it but their 'interior condition,' the inner place from which they operate or the *source* from which all of their actions originate."

Continue your interior exploration and ask yourself, "Who am I?" Aspiring or experienced principals may be shaking their heads, muttering, "I don't need this psychological stuff!" Yes, you do. This question and your answers are at the root of your leadership efficacy. You can glance in a mirror to see if there is a smudge on your face or you can really peer at that glass and try to figure out who is "behind the mask." Kouzes and Posner, authors *of A Leader's Legacy*, believe that "people always want to know something about the person doing the leading before they are going to become the people doing the following. They want to know what is behind the mask." Because change is part of everything in life, this is a question that should be asked more than once. A baseline response from you at age thirty is only the beginning of your leadership journey; experiences and enlightenment over the years should reveal even more self-knowledge, which will strengthen your leadership effectiveness. Kouzes and Posner also write, "All serious leadership starts from within. That's the only way we will ever be able to respond to what our constituents most expect and want from us. And what is that? What they most want from us is that we be genuinely who we are."

Linger a bit longer in this line of thinking, and ponder what brings you joy. Some people stumble through life and seem surprised when happiness is theirs, others know what makes them smile, feel glad, and work to make this happen frequently. None of us can escape pain in this life—it is real and sometimes constant, but we can scatter instances of joy throughout our day or week to help us function better.

Emotionally secure people recognize what makes them feel warm and lighthearted. If you don't really know what brings you joy, now is the time to think about it. Get out paper and a pencil and recall the times when you were content and at peace with the world. Your list will not be like another's, which is as it should be; we are all unique. With this list in hand, make an effort to recapture some of these moments of joy. For most of us, the simple pleasures are the ones we return to again and again because they work. As a principal, you will have your share of pain, angst, and troubles. It is your job, however, to counteract these assaults by infusing joy into the picture. This will help you do a better job of leading and will influence the behavior of your staff members and teachers, which will in turn affect students' attitudes and performance.

Do some more soul-searching and decide whether to drown in emotions or not. We are all awash in emotions from time to time; it is one of the dramatic things that makes us human. It is freeing, however, to realize that we have some control; we do not have to become a slave to our feelings. Jill Bolte Taylor, a brain anatomist who suffered a severe stroke, has taught us much through her illness and her insights. In *A Brain Scientist's Personal Journey*, she writes, "One of the greatest lessons I learned was how to feel the physical component of emotion. Joy was a feeling in my body. Peace was a feeling in my body. I thought it was interesting that I could feel new emotions flood through me and then release me. I had to learn new words to label these 'feeling' experiences, and most remarkably, I learned that I had the power to choose whether to hook into a feeling and prolong its presence in my body, or just let it quickly flow right out of me."

Ken, a young chairman of the board at a private school, who did not go through such a devastating experience as Bolton Taylor had, was nonetheless wise beyond his years when he said to a school head facing a particular situation, "I hope you don't choose to remain angry." What a gift of insight this was to a leader. As human beings, we will experience emotions, positive and negative, but we do not have to become victims of prolonged pain. Principals must be emotionally balanced to envision a path and inspire others to follow along.

MASTERMINDING AN APPROACH

Most exemplary leaders spend a good deal of time thinking before they act. To the outside observer, they may seem to come through chaos unscathed, which may not be the true picture. While they may not have had any prior notice of a particular chaotic event, they probably have been preparing themselves for years to be calm in times of crisis. These admirable leaders are not reactionaries; they are planners. Planning takes intentionality and insight. If you want to make wise decisions, you need to make time for meaning. A principal's life is hectic; things are hurled at you so often and so rapidly that for the most part, you just take in information and file the issue somewhere in your brain to deal with later. This "later" needs to be fit into your life or else you will miss the essence of what is important. There are various ways to schedule this thinking, and they all usually involve getting out of the school environment to do your best work.

Going on a leadership retreat helps clear the fog and can inspire next steps. Writing in a journal identifies problems and frequently uncovers solutions that seemed hidden. Being outside and doing something pleasurable, such as walking a trail with your dog or sitting in a garden alone, stills the sounds that stifle your creative spirit. Find a system that works for you.

You may not be facing a particular problem at the moment, but be purposeful and make room each day for pockets of silence. Even if you are a social being who is stimulated by others, you need time alone. Self-reflection and self-renewal, which pave the way for growth, are only possible when centered and still. You can find these pockets of silence anywhere. The key is to allow yourself the luxury of doing nothing for a period of time. As a principal, you will have a perpetually full calendar, so finding this pocket of silence routinely requires perseverance. If you find it impossible to sit quietly alone, which many type-A school heads do, consider attending a group meditation, which can help with technique and focus. The practice of meditation, an ancient ritual in many faith traditions, is enjoying resurgence among believers and nonbelievers for its power to settle the mind and bring calm amid chaos. If you are curious, consult the Internet for meditation groups in your area or research the books and apps available.

Besides considering meditation, find other ways to relieve anxiety. Denying that it is there is just putting your head in a rabbit hole. Being a school leader is stressful; so brainstorm ways to relieve stress that will work for you. Try tap dance or line dance, play Frisbee with your dog, join a fantasy football league, or take up scrapbooking. The answer is finding an activity or hobby that is healthy, wholesome, and briefly takes you into another world where you are not a decision-maker for a school. Principals with compulsive tendencies who believe they have to work 24–7 often make poor decisions and eventually burn out. School leaders in general are notorious workaholics, so to help you balance your professional and personal life, develop a daily exit strategy.

At a meeting of the National Advisory Board of the Harvard's Principals' Center, each member discussed his or her routine schedule. Regardless of the school, these extraordinary leaders disclosed that they normally worked twelve-hour days and often went into school on the weekend. You cannot work this schedule without some system in place to keep you sane. Some school administrators with children in day care have a built-in "excuse" to leave before the center closes at six. Of course, these principals frequently work well into the night once their young children are asleep. Some principals change into athletic gear and head for the school track at sunset and then return to their desks to resume working. One new principal from Wyoming, sensing the endless demands placed before her as a school leader, was creative. When asked how she remained calm and collected, she replied, "Get a horse. Cats and dogs can often fend for themselves," she said, "but a horse cannot." Her horse needed to be fed and exercised at the end of each day, so she had her own exit strategy. She too probably worked at home after her stable work, but the break gave her a physical, mental, and emotional release, enabling her to function better. Most city and suburban school heads don't have this luxury of owning a horse, but they too need to find their own system for getting out the door before bedtime.

People can help you stay centered if you choose wisely. Seek companions who are likeminded and positive. When times are tough, you need people around you who can hold you up and help you cope. But don't be content to stick just with these folks. When all is calm, search for people who can stretch you, causing you to look at the world differently. As you go about your day, notice the little things that cross your path and make you smile. Listening to the chorus rehearse and nail a new number, welcoming a school-phobic middle-school student when he arrives in the morning, or seeing a normally testy parent pay a compliment to a coach are fuel for your next steps as a leader. Remember kindnesses, and savor the sweetness. It will alter your outlook on life and define your actions as a principal. Leaders have to develop conscious ways to avoid becoming cantankerous and callous.

ACTING WITH INTENTION

Energize by engaging with students each day. They are the reason for your being. Let them rejuvenate you and remind you of your purpose. Formal and informal exchanges are important. Experienced principals admit that the students they spend the most time with are usually found at both ends of the spectrum—the very successful, who are winning awards, and those who are not successful and are waging war with the system either by acting out or by withdrawing. Meet with these students from both extremes. Those doing well need less of your time—a pat on the back and a few congratulatory words are all that it takes to keep them plugging away. Spend extra time with those who are struggling. They may have met with teachers, advisors, and counselors to no avail, but you have to give it your best shot as well. Usually, unsuccessful students are sullen and silent when meeting adults. You have to break this pattern if you want to have any chance of helping them. One middle-school principal kept an assortment of balls in her office, numerous squishy tennis balls and bigger textured balls that actually lit up when squeezed. When dialogue stalled with some of these students who were hurting, she would just go to her cabinet without a word, select a ball, toss it to the surprised student, and then quietly participate in a "game" of catch. Sometimes after a bit, there would be a natural opening and conversation could begin, other times, the surprise of playing ball in the principal's office was only a first step toward communication at a later date. To connect with those students who fill up the wide space between these two extremes, eat in the cafeteria some days, sit in the student section of the bleachers at a game, or go to recess. You need them, and they need you.

Because your life as a school head is inherently active and full of chaotic moments, you have to resist the urge to cope by relying on automatic pilot. When this happens, people notice that the passion is gone and then they too begin to lose interest. You don't have to be an extrovert bubbling over with enthusiasm every minute, but you do have to be present for each exchange and alert to everything going on around you. How is this possible? Start with your best centering tool: your body. Breathe deeply. Shallow breaths don't do the job and only increase anxiety. Your body needs deep, cleansing breaths to oxygenate your entire system. At one back-to-school orientation, a yoga instructor was brought in by the head of school to illustrate some ways to relieve stress. In addition to walking them through yoga poses, she taught employees how to breathe properly, particularly when feeling anxious. Using a thumb and little finger to block specific nasal passages, she demonstrated how to inhale through one nostril only and exhale through the other nostril. This procedure was funny at first, but gradually people began to see that it worked. Perhaps, more importantly, teachers and staff members began to realize that they were in charge of managing their own stress and thus the stress of students.

Stress is often brought about by the unsettling feeling that our lives are out of control, that things are falling through the cracks, and that we are somehow failing to do our jobs well. This is not surprising, particularly for a principal who has more agendas to manage and appointments to keep than seem humanly possible. Rather than succumb to this potentially numbing condition, which can injure an individual psyche and affect an entire school community, employ a simple administrative technique recommended by corporate consultant David Allen called, "What's the next action?" This can work easily for mundane personal things that need to be done, such as making a dental appointment to more complex professional projects that involve groups, such as designing a school building.

Despite the value of many heads puzzling over a problem and the benefit of collaborative problem solving, an unsettling persistent randomness can reign if the leader is not in control using proven techniques to manage the people involved and the activity that flows from their togetherness. Creativity has its place in problem solving and planning, but to keep chaos at bay and run a healthy and productive organization, action steps need to be employed regularly. If you lead with this approach, your stress will diminish, and others in the school community will begin to imitate your approach. Allen states, "When a culture adopts 'What's the next action?' as a standard operating query, there's an automatic increase in energy, productivity, clarity, and focus." Ask yourself, "What's the next action?" when your personal life seems like it is unraveling. This subtle shift will move you from being overwhelmed to being more in control. At the end of meetings, ask the key question, "What's the next action?" and then as the dialogue ensues, determine tasks and timelines.

Now use your mind as a centering tool. Read something every day to make you stretch. The shorter the piece, the better, for you will find the few minutes to do it and the pithiness will give you time to ponder its meaning in your life. A book of quotations on your desk or bedside table is one way to achieve this goal. As you get into the habit, you may find you want more from a specific writer or a particular topic, and you'll delve deeper. A principal must inspire others. This requires a constant filling of one's own well. Another way to combat chaos and gain perspective on life is doing hands-on work for people in need. Whether it is stacking cans in a soup kitchen, pushing wheelchairs in a nursing home, or delivering meals, you will be humbled, and your seemingly serious problems as a principal will fade a bit into the background. Don't think you are too busy; this kind of involvement will actually help you do your job better.

Little problems and big problems will fill up your days as a principal. If you approach these challenges of the job with intentionality, your life will easier and you will do a better job of leading. Decide as a school head to forget personal verbal attacks. At one time or another, someone in pain or in anger will call you "overbearing," "insensitive," "irrational," or "insane." These may be some of the kinder names you will be called. Turn the other cheek, and don't harbor resentment once the air is cleared and the problem is addressed. Realizing that encounters can become ugly if you let them, sort out your feelings before you enter a potentially confrontational meeting. Sometimes this is not possible; a situation will spring up that needs immediate attention, but if you can, delay a meeting that you suspect will be full of conflict. You want time to settle down and get your emotions under control so you can deal with the real issues in the case. Waiting a day usually does the trick.

If you want to stay centered and do your best work as a leader, gather information and take time to mull over the facts before you make a difficult decision. Get advice from trusted colleagues or advisors. At times, you may have to consult the central office, the board, or an attorney before coming to a conclusion. You don't want to drag out a decision, but you want to be as sure as you can that you came to this conclusion impartially and intelligently. Michael Useem, business-school professor, researcher, and author of *The Go Point*, states, "Poor preparation predictably leads to poor choices." He realizes, however, that there is no perfect situation for decision-making and subscribes to the 70 percent solution based on the Marine Corps system of "training officers to make decisions when they are 70 percent confident of the outcome." This is an ideal approach for school leaders, but that being said, expect to function alone at times. Although sometimes you will have the luxury of conferencing as needed, there will be other critical times when you have to step up to the plate and lead without a phalanx behind you.

The attacks on the United States on 9/11 are one such example. On campuses large and small, principals had to do what they thought best for their students and their employees without dithering. When the members of the National Advisory Board for the Principals Center at the Graduate School of Education at Harvard University met in Cambridge only weeks later, it was astounding that each principal sitting around the oval table discussed similar actions taken on his or her campus. Principals jumped into gear; they did not call the central office or supervisory board for advice. They just did what needed to be done to manage fears and ensure safety at their schools. Many of these leaders in their singular focus forgot their own families who were firefighters in New York or citizens in our capital city, Washington, D.C. This is how real leaders function in a face of an emergency.

While others may cause you to believe that you are indispensable, you are not. To remain centered and focused on the mission, take a day off when necessary. Teachers take mental health days when they are feeling wrung out and stay home when they have a bad cold; you can too. Most school heads are so conscientious that they feel guilty taking any time off, even when it would be wise to do so. The last thing a principal wants to do is collapse from the flu at a meeting or be so stressed and tired that poor decisions are being made. You may be surprised how well your school can function even if you are not there. A day in your bathrobe at home can do wonders for your mental and physical health.

To be an influential school leader, you cannot throw up your hands in the midst of swirling chaos. As the person at the center of the school community, others will take their cue from you. You are the one who has to maintain order, calm, and civility despite minor skirmishes and major attacks. To do this, you need a game plan. Of course, your vision, implementation, and calendar matter enormously. These are the threads running through the day-to-day life of a school that will strengthen its chance of success for student achievement. Your game plan, however, has to acknowledge the reality of disequilibrium, which can slow progress or stop it for a time. Adaptive leaders recognize the unpredictability of our world but nonetheless are undaunted and learn to manage chaos and lead others through tunnels of darkness into the light. To combat chaos, you need to have strong proactive programs in place to lessen destruction. Consider the health, safety, and security procedures for every avenue of the school's operation to be sacrosanct. Every drill has the potential to save a life; every procedure can lessen the pain for an individual or the school as a whole. Your game plan for dealing with chaos also has to include your personal life as well, including practices that enable you to lead with unfaltering purpose and focused energy.

Six

Flexing Ethical Muscle

SETTING A PERSONAL COMPASS

It isn't possible to make a rule for every situation that a child will face, so although most parents and teachers have logical consequences for misbehavior—a time-out chair, extra chores, or withdrawing a privilege—the real goal is to have a child grasp and accept what is socially acceptable and what is not. We cannot follow youngsters everywhere, so we want them to have good behavior whether we are watching them or not. Ask any parent: squabbles occur when they're on the phone or in the shower. Ask any teacher: the real test of a school's culture and discipline policy is what goes on in the hallways between classes or at recess when adult eyes cannot possibly take in everything. Internalizing goodness and right reactions to daily life in all of its complexity are what disciplined children personify.

Fast forward several decades. We want this same discipline in our spouses, our neighbors, our colleagues, and especially in our leaders. In adults, we consider this disciplined behavior ethics. At its core, leadership is unpredictable. It is impossible to list all of the rules, and, in addition, we are not even capable of imagining future scenarios that a president or principal might have to face. Because of this uncertainty, we cannot rely on specific if-then policies; rather, we must look at the person who will be making the decisions. Character is at the center.

Regardless of any past indiscretions in our youth, as adults, we now are required to be ethical in every way possible. Morally, you can't be casual about what you stand for and expect in the school environment. This commitment has to go with the territory and title. To the best of your ability, you have to be consistently honest, trustworthy, and fair. You have to balance the good of the individual with the good of the whole, and always be on the lookout for how to help the other fellow. Your conscience, a reflection of the moral law, is that little whisper that tells you what is right and encourages you to act thusly even when no one is looking. Some of these whispers will tell you what not to do—don't spread rumors, don't compromise testing protocols, don't lie about school finances—and some of these whispers will tell you what to do—treat others fairly, including the pesky ones; operate as transparently as possible; give a good day's work for a good day's pay. Your conscience is always lurking in the background, ready to assist in decision-making if you quiet yourself and listen. A personal compass is proactive and sets the direction for your actions from the start.

As you try to determine how best to set your personal compass, consider the North Star. In history, religion, and leadership studies, this remarkable stationary star has guided countless explorers on land and on sea. Its brilliance beckons to those who look skyward, and its constancy never ceases to amaze stargazers. You need to find your own North Star and define its points of light. Bill George and Peter Sims, authors of *True North: Discover your Authentic Leadership*, believe that while you can learn from others, to be truly successful, you must be your best self. Joe, a big Texan, wore his cowboy boots to Harvard meetings and rode his motorcycle to school visits whenever possible. That didn't diminish his exemplary status as a high-school principal one bit. He was sure of himself without being cocky, and everyone around him was comfortable in his authenticity.

That kind of presence means being honest with yourself and with others. A particularly apt colloquial expression from the West "Big hat, no cattle" sums up what other people think of those who imitate or merely posture.

Because you now know the importance of being authentic, you have to resist the urge to be popular. Surely you want to be accepted and liked, but popularity is not your goal. You will have to make decisions that sometimes will not please students, faculty, staff, and parents. Be resolute but not rude during these rocky times, and know that leadership is never easy. If you can convince the school community that your decisions are made thoughtfully, impartially, and with everyone's best interest in mind, you will at least be respected, if not loved.

Stephen Covey, author of many leadership books, believes setting your compass is more important than reading a map; it is helpful to create your own touchstone. Problems are frequently complex and more gray than black and white. A simple test in decision-making should always be in the forefront of your mind. A question like "Is this in the best interest of students?" puts everything into perspective. You also want to develop an integrity query that works for you alone. It could be "Would I want this information about me to be shared with my children, told to my grand-mother, or published on the front page of the *New York Times*?"

Positions of power get many people into hot water because notably higher salaries, coveted parking spaces, coffee coming on demand, and too much adulation can make people believe they are above the law or the standards of an ethical world. Melinda was a principal on the move. She had degrees from Ivy League universities and thus was sought after by struggling schools that felt she had a magic wand that could transform failure into success. If the schools had looked carefully at her résumé, however, they might have noticed that she rarely remained at a school more than two or three years. That was because Melinda was focused on Melinda primarily and it took a while for school communities to figure this out. The perks of the position were what motivated her. She wielded power ruthlessly within her own domain and thought she could do the same in any other setting, which startled and soon alienated people. Melinda spoke of her impor-tance to anyone within earshot. Her obsession with getting a six-figure salary and having a premier parking space became the ethical albatross that eventually doomed her as an educational leader. While most school heads are not this power crazed and unprincipled, they do exist. Perhaps no one ever reminded these individuals of the extraordinary ethical responsibility conferred upon educational administrators. Or maybe they just got stuck in the egocentric lifestyles of adolescents.

Becoming an ethical person requires maturity. Figuring out who you are and what you believe in moves you out of that self-centered place we all occupied as teenagers. A lively conscience, a personal compass, a centering touchstone, and a sense of integrity will serve you well if you want to be a true leader. Before you get mired in real ethical dilemmas, mull over potential breaches of trust. In your position as principal, you are given guidelines but also latitude. School policy states that "credit-card receipts are to be submitted to the finance office promptly," but it is up to you to be aboveboard and not submit a bill for taking your cousin out to dinner. Office supplies are generously given as needed to administrators at school, but it is assumed that these are to serve office work only. You, as a school head, must be scrupulous about buying your own staplers and scissors for home use.

Clark was a young principal sent to a leadership conference in an attractive city. A senior school head he ran into admitted to a group of fellow educators at the hotel check-in line that he never actually attended any sessions at conference meetings and tried to persuade Clark and others to join him for a round of golf at a nearby resort. Clark was both flattered by the attention and conflicted. He knew his school had paid for the conference and the travel, and the program looked promising. As a relative greenhorn, Clark was looking forward to learning more about data-driven initiatives and systems for creating safe schools inside and out, but the thought of tooling around manicured fairways with some big guns seemed an impossible dream. Fortunately, his personal compass directed him to do the honorable thing. He politely declined the golf outing and went to the meetings. You will never be sorry for your ethical stance. On the other hand, small slips of trustworthiness often lead to more serious moral offenses.

Avoid at all costs the self-indulgent trap of "I am owed this." Everyone sinks to this level occasionally, particularly when tired or stressed, but a school head cannot allow this fleeting dark cloud of self-pity to be actualized in some bizarre behavior. You are owed nothing beyond what is in your contract—not extra money, materials, vacation, benefits, perks, or privileges. Leaders who embarrass themselves, humiliate family members, and betray the trust of the public are those people who succumb to this kind of thinking and commit illegal or immoral acts. Principals beware. In your leadership journey, be sure to connect the dots between your professional and your personal life. What you say publicly to the press, the community, your colleagues, and the students, you must live privately.

USING A COMPASS TO GUIDE RELATIONSHIPS

Being a principal involves frequent and intense contact with others. Kindergarten students are eager to demonstrate their new decoding skills to you; middle-school students hope you will stop by and admire their decorations for the dance; and high-school students, too cool to ask, really want you in the front row at their theater productions and basketball games. Each faculty and staff member hungers for a piece of you as well. They want you to know about their professional challenges—the child in a fifth-grade class who shows some signs of neglect, the parent who complains each season about athletic coaching techniques, and the abysmal reading-comprehension scores of the incoming freshman class. They also want to share their victories—a child who had been rejected by peers finally integrating into a class, improved test scores in math, and a successful field trip with students and parents on their best behavior. In addition, their personal challenges and victories will often be shared with you, and while never prying, you must be available to listen as needed. You are their leader. Teacher and staff members have a personal as well as a professional life, and sometimes they need to lean on you or hear your kudos. Be available.

Periodically, it will seem as if you are really running a school for parents and not children. Parents will call you, e-mail you, send notes to you, or be at your door with minor concerns and major problems. Your compass will have to be handy as you work with them. Parents are usually tense in your presence, even at PTA meetings or fundraisers when their child is not the actual focus. Principals bring back scary memories for most people. In these public instances, do all you can to be friendly and accessible to everyone. In more private meetings where parents are concerned about their children, you must be open and not defensive. While you need to beware of not promising them the moon, parents need to believe that you have heard their complaints and at the very least will consider the issues. Teary and visibly shaken parents may bring out the best in you. Your maternal or paternal streak will surge forth, and you will want to right every wrong in their path. Rude and demanding parents, on the other hand, may make your blood boil and force you to bite your tongue to resist acting as they do. Both kinds of parents and even those in between these two extremes can get you off course if you are not careful. When faced with parental issues and emotions, let your true North Star guide you and steer the conversation back to the child in question and possible solutions.

If you have been called a "people person," be grateful for the gift, because it may be easier for you to relate to so many people. Even if you are an introvert at heart, however, you have to push yourself to become a connector. As a principal, your relationships don't end with students, employees, and parents. They extend to professional colleagues in other schools, regulatory agencies, supervisory personnel, and members of the community. Your manner of dealing with these people must reflect the same standards you initially set for yourself. In all of these relationships, respect for others is the basis of your exchanges. As the leader in the school, expect this same approach in others, and insist that consideration be shown to everyone. There are no exceptions here. Respect should be an attitude deeply felt and best shown by outward gestures of good manners and kindness. If there is a culture of disrespect on your campus, don't hesitate to institute a civility code for students, teachers, staff members, and parents with consequences for violations. It will improve behavior and the school climate. This code does not replace any discipline policies in place but goes to the core of the problem, recognizing each person as a fellow human being and responding with consideration.

From this basic respect, trust should flow. You will build trust one action at a time, one person at a time. Gradually, this trust will be banked, which is critical when difficult decisions are required. Trust does not come with the title *principal*; you have to earn it. In fact, more often it is distrust that you will encounter early on. It may not be ugly and in-your-face suspicion, but it is there, silently stalking you until your behavior consistently tips the scales in favor of credibility. Be patient with yourself and the community. Showing that you're truly principled takes time for others to absorb.

When you are sure that you have based your relationships on respect, have insisted that this be part of the school culture, and have begun to feel a foundation of trust underfoot, it is tempting for a school head to get too comfortable with others and, therefore, slip personally. Watch your more casual exchanges. Joke prudently with colleagues, students, and parents, and take great care that humor and fun never become inappropriate or ugly. Discrimination should never be part of any humorous remark; this includes discrimination based on race, religion, size, gender, culture, or anything else that could hurt an individual. Clearly, as a school leader you are held to a very high standard as a speaker in this regard, but, in addition, if you are present when an insensitive remark is made that is discriminatory or in bad taste, it is your job to step up to the plate and say, "This is not appropriate; this is not what we laugh at on this campus." Don't be afraid to take a moral stand.

Also encourage your employees to avoid using sarcasm with students. It is a technique that some teachers, thinking they are humorous, employ as a teaching tool. This is a bad idea. It always inflicts pain, even when students disguise the hurt. Barry, a good-natured principal, joked and teased everyone in sight but did not always notice the puzzled reactions to his remarks. Peer-to-peer sparring is pretty common in the workplace, but a principal's flippant comment intended to be funny can be interpreted entirely differently. When this happens, the teacher or staff member may stop dead in her tracks and wonder, "Now what in the world did he mean by that?" Principals who have recently moved from faculty status to CEO have to be sure to make this subtle shift in their exchanges. Even with a pure heart, leaders cannot afford to send out mixed messages.

In your relationships with professional colleagues, beware of the green-eyed monster: jealousy. Healthy competition is good for schools and education in general, but when mean-spirited conversations and persistent grudges become the norm, it is sweet competition gone sour. Help those you work with grasp this distinction and model a mature attitude. Be the first to call your rival high school that won the basketball tournament. Send a note to a principal in your district who was selected as Principal of the Year. This shows you are a person of integrity with a generous spirit.

ADOPTING AN ETHICS AND INTEGRITY POLICY

You want to be sure that your behavior and all of the happenings in the school community are reflections of an ethics policy that is broad enough to include all possible ethical matters while narrow enough to identify specific behaviors that are expected. One of your many tasks is to identify this policy and make it viable. If you are panicking, don't. You don't have to be a trained ethician or start from scratch. What you have to do is some research. Most likely, there is an ethics and integrity policy that you are already expected to follow or there is one that you can adopt for your school. The National Education Association, (NEA) has a Code of

Ethics for educators that includes a "Commitment to the Student" and a "Commitment to the Profession." If you are a principal in a public school, your state or local school board may have a policy for schools to follow. The American Association of School Administrators (AASA) has a code of ethics for educational leaders. If you are a school head in a private school, begin by reading *Principles for Good Governance and Ethical Practice: A Guide for Charities and Foundations*, assembled by the Panel on the Nonprofit Sector. While this is not intended directly for schools, it is complete and clear in its guidelines and should start you off in the right direction. The National Association of Independent Schools (NAIS) has promulgated "Principles of Good Practice" for its member schools. The American Montessori Society has established a code of ethics for its schools. Most faith-based schools have extensive ethics and integrity policies developed by central boards or dioceses that individual schools are expected to follow.

In all of these instances, oftentimes policies exist but are not made public by the principal or considered part of the daily life of schooling. They tend to be stuck in some administrative file without ever being exposed to the light of day. Do your homework. Find out what policies apply to your school. If you find that your school does not have an umbrella ethics and integrity policy covering it, create one with help from your governing board using guidelines from more established organizations. It is foolhardy for start-up schools, charter schools, or cyber schools to ignore this crucial organizational piece or for any school, for that matter, to consider policies for ethics and integrity as mere institutional documents or burdensome red tape binding the hands of educators. On the contrary, all of these policies, regardless of their origin, define the true nature of education, assert the dignity of every human being, and spell out the rights and responsibilities of those involved in the process.

Even while noting their similarities, each ethics and integrity policy will vary in scope and detail. Attention to the student is addressed by all policies and usually begins by claiming a student's right to an education that will enable him or her to utilize potential and become a self-sustaining member of society. As you scan various codes, specifics included in the different policies should help you grasp the gravity of a code of ethics for your school. In the NEA Code of Ethics, under Principle I, Commitment to the Student, # 5, "In fulfillment of the obligation to the student, the educator—shall not intentionally expose the student to embarrassment or discouragement." How often do you suppose this essential policy is discussed with teachers? The Catholic Diocese of Charlotte, North Carolina, in its *Policy of Ethics and Integrity: Guidelines Working with Minor Children* states, "Church personnel [includes teachers] are not to speak to minor children in a manner that is or could be construed by an observer as derogatory, demeaning, threatening, intimidating or humiliating, and are not to use profane or foul language in the presence of minor children." Wouldn't you want this part of a code of ethics in your school? Protecting students from physical and sexual abuse in schools is incorporated into many ethic codes. Some educational organizations and school systems require attendance at an ethics and integrity seminar that covers topics such having appropriate and inappropriate physical contact with students, showing suitable emotional engagement, setting boundaries in dealing with students, and reporting suspected abuse. Follow up on this topic and make sure your employees are educated and your students are protected.

In your research, be clear about the distinction between legal and ethical responsibilities. Laws mandate or prohibit certain behaviors. If you are a public-school administrator, have a copy of the classic *American Public School Law* by brothers Kern and M. David Alexander in your office for quick referral. Even if your district provides legal counsel, you are responsible for knowing potential issues and possible pitfalls. Private schools are not subject to many of same laws as public schools, but nevertheless, you need to be informed of your school's responsibility. A handbook from NAIS, *Policies for Independent Schools: Acting Legally and Accountably in Today's Changing Environment* by Debra P. Wilson and Eileen Johnson, may help nonpublic school heads understand issues. Laws carry sanctions in the courts. Ethics carry sanctions in accrediting agencies, membership organizations, and in individual school communities. Although the focus here is on adopting an ethics and integrity policy for your school, you cannot ignore your own ethical responsibility as a principal. You, as a school head, have to be diligent in seeing that your school is in legal compliance with all applicable laws.

Many departments in your school community will be governed by ethics polices tailored to a particular discipline. Admissions, accounting, athletics, counseling, fund-raising, library science, and special education all have codes of behavior and guidelines for practice. Again, some of these policies will be general in scope. The American School Counselors Association states in its Ethical Standards for School Counselors, "The professional school counselor has a primary obligation to the student, who is to be treated with respect as a unique individual." And some will be all inclusive, such as *The Rules and Regulations Governing Athletics, A Handbook for Principals and Athletic Directors.* These principals and athletic directors are from schools that are members of the Massachusetts Interscholastic Athletic Association. In addition to identifying and publicizing a code of ethics for the entire school community, as principal you want to be knowledgeable about specific codes governing departments in the school. Create a file to include each discipline's code that you will refer to from time to time while administering a school. Complaints from a parent about unequal playing time in athletics were quickly dealt with by one school head whose savvy athletic director, Jody, made sure the principal was familiar with the league rules governing playing time for various skill levels of teams. A grading challenge in another school concerning the use of source material without documentation was resolved by referring to a class a student had attended that focused on copyright laws and responsibilities and was taught by experienced and ethical librarians.

Whether you are in a public or a private school, as a principal, you will be dealing with school boards in some way. As a school head, you want to be aware of the code of ethics governing these partners in education. Read the applicable codes not with an intent to trip up opponents but with a desire to understand the roles and responsibilities of your partnership. It can be enlightening reading. Pine Island Public School District #255 has a *Board Members Code of Ethics Policy* that is refreshing and direct. Part I. begins, "As a member of the Board I will: A. Listen. B. Recognize the integrity of my predecessors and associates. C. Appreciate the merit of their work." There are six other sections dealing with particular policies, but the prudent and practical beginning of this policy sets the tone for ethical and efficient collaborative work. If you are head of a private school that has frequent trustee turnover, gently guide the board chair to documents that may be useful in orienting new trustees and facilitating productive meetings and decisions making. Lynne, a new board chair, had a copy of the "Code of Ethics for Catholic School Board Members" inserted into each trustee's binder and was read before meetings. This helped focus the work ahead, which could get sidelined by even the most well-intentioned volunteers.

In researching and amassing ethical policies to consider, you will begin to realize the scope of issues to address. Review your school policies for hiring and firing, harassment, student records, testing, discipline, retirement, insurance, compensation, financial aid, performance evaluations, financial management, grievances, whistle blowing, and conflict of interest, just to mention some of the ethical arenas you need to explore. A number of these topics will be included in your student and/or employee handbooks; however, your ethics and integrity policy must highlight the rationale, rights, and responsibilities and be in sync with the specifics in the handbooks. Just as you will want to review your handbooks yearly, you will want to review your ethics policy as well. The basic approach should not change; however, you want to be sure that your policy reflects any new challenges that may exist for members functioning in an ethical group setting. Evolving technology is a case in point. At the appropriate time, after you have given sufficient study to the topic at hand, the ethics-and-integrity policy should be publicly displayed, promoted by you, and endorsed by everyone in the school community.

EMPLOYING ETHICAL POLICIES

A bit of clarification may help here. Ethics is defined as "a set of principles of right conduct." Integrity is "steadfast adherence to a strict ethical code" (*American Heritage Dictionary*). It is not enough to have established a code of ethics; you must now put the principles into practice and inspire others to do the same. Like it or not, members of the school community will look to you for standards of ethical behavior. Everything you do or say must reflect an authentic moral constitution. A genuine sense of right and wrong and consistent application of these principles are what makes us truly human and worthy of leadership. Make it a point to keep promises. Whether you agree to bring a dish to the potluck faculty party, write a college recommendation, or pledge a donation to help the band go to a national competition, be true to your word. Saying "yes" to an appeal is the easy part, and sometimes you will wish you hadn't been such an easy sell; however, people are counting on you and watching to see if you will honor your commitment. No matter how insignificant, a promise is a sacred word, that when kept contributes to character or when brushed off becomes part of a downward spiral ending in disgrace.

Your followers will be listening as well as looking at your behavior; therefore, you want to speak the same truth to all stakeholders. Everyone deserves the facts and you as a school head must not speak out of both sides of your mouth. If the reason that you abandoned the German program was because enrollment was down and you could not afford to offer a class for eight students, admit it. If the reason you hired an intern for the primary grades was to make your instructional groups smaller, which would affect achievement, admit it. If the reason you instituted a school-uniform policy was to improve student behavior, admit it. Sometimes a school head cannot divulge reasons for actions to protect the privacy of personnel, parents or students; however, whenever the facts don't compromise individuals, the public should hear the same story.

Like doctors, lawyers, therapists, and religious leaders, you are called to protect individuals and preserve privileged information. You must keep confidences confidential—period. Because of your position, you will be privy to all kinds of personal information. You will know whose check for the overnight field trip bounced, whose teenage daughter just found out she is pregnant, whose husband lost his job, and who is on medication for depression. A surefire way to hijack your professional career, to cause incredible heartbreak to a colleague, or to encourage malicious gossip in the school community is to talk or even drop hints about a tragic situation. This also goes for the temptation to share private information with your trusted administrative assistant or your sympathetic bed partner—forget it; mum is the word for an ethical principal.

In addition to protecting individuals, be discreet in all matters. As a sitting principal, everyone will pump you for information. The budget, a new employee, curriculum changes, student transfers, the calendar, an athletic team, and the school board will be just a few of the topics that people will try to discuss with you. This is easy to resist in more formal sessions during meetings or in your office, but watch those informal times, at the concession stand or in the grocery store, when you let your guard down and don't even realize that you are being interrogated. Then it is too late; a rumor will circulate before you reach your driveway: "Dr. Jones thinks the new superintendent is slow to respond to issues" or "Mrs. Parker is also concerned about the number of juniors on the JV soccer team." News, real or fictitious, flows through school campuses faster than CNN. Don't become the source of gossip. It will always come back to haunt you.

When thinking about your own moral code, it is wise to watch the free lunches. In your role as a school leader, you will have many invitations. Some of these are part of the job—meetings with your boss, committees, and community groups—and most of the time someone else will pick up the check, which is OK; your position is being honored. You also will receive other invitations for coffee, lunch, or dinner, and you must always be alert as to why. "Why is this person or this group courting me, and if I say yes and accept their offer, will I be beholden to them?" Astute leaders are constantly attentive to the reasons for "free lunches" that take them away from school where the real work is being done. Don't get too comfortable with being taken care of; with your colleagues on campus, you are just one of the bananas in the bunch. If your school has a cafeteria, pay your own way rather than assume you get a free lunch as principal. If your school has parties to cover incidentals or cheer projects, be sure to be the first person to contribute.

Finance is an area where ethical principles and practices often collide. In the world of commerce and public service, the public is frequently disappointed by leaders' promises that fall flat or by personal behaviors that belie ethical policies. Schools, unfortunately, are not exempt either, and the media delights in highlighting every ethical disaster like when a charter school closes suddenly for lack of fiscal oversight and students are left stranded, or when a coach in a private school is arrested for skimming off monies from athletic fees and the school struggles to find ways to offer the sport and pay coaching stipends. Students in both settings suffer, and education in general becomes suspect. You as principal must see financial matters in your school as a moral responsibility. Begin with any personal accounting. Avoid commingling personal and professional expenses. Often a principal will be given a school credit card to use for travel, emergencies, and nonroutine purchases. If you are in the grocery store picking up a cake for a school celebration and you realize you need a quart of milk for home, don't be tempted to combine this shopping on the school credit card, even if you fully intend to pay the school back. It is messy, can be misunderstood by others, and is ethically murky.

Be rigorous about overseeing all budgetary and financial transactions. Depending upon the nature of the school (public, charter, or private), the financial obligations of the principal will vary, but in all cases, there will be some fiscal oversight necessary. When this does not happen, or when it happens haphazardly, a school is at risk, and students suffer. If a significant part of your job is managing finances, particularly in a charter or an independent school, be sure you have adequate training in preparing, understanding, and monitoring budgets. If you were a liberal arts major and feel insecure dealing with business matters, take a seminar to become more adept at working with numbers. Be sure in any school that you have clearly articulated policies for handling monies on campus. Basic procedures should be institutionalized; the person preparing checks for accounts payable should not be the check signer. All requests for checks should have accompanying receipts, including credit-card payments. Bills should be paid on time to avoid penalties. Bank deposits should be made daily, two people should always record monies coming into the school, and a locked deposit box secured to a wall or a safe should be used for deposits. Limit the occasions when cash is exchanged; this is an open invitation for fraud. Books fairs, field trips, athletic uniform sales, and PTA events are all venues where cash is likely to be on hand. When it is necessary to have funds exchanged, always have two or more people present. As checks come in, they should be stamped "For Deposit Only" and cash should be counted and documented several times daily. If an event continues over several days, the shoebox or portable cashbox used as a bank should be emptied into a locked safe as soon as it is full. There should never be cash or checks left unattended at a school. Don't take your fiscal responsibilities lightly. You may get support from your own finance office, the superintendent, the district, a finance committee, or an audit committee, but, as head of a school, you are responsible. In any organization, financial oversight and ethical behavior are closely aligned.

To insure continual high standards of ethics and integrity concerning finances in your school, have an annual fraud analysis performed. Joe, an easygoing gentleman with a perpetual smile, was a lead partner in a reputable accounting firm who performed an external audit for an independent school without a glitch. Then one year he asked the school head, the controller, and a board member from the finance committee to fill out a fraud analysis. What an initially daunting request! Why? While there was never any indication of fraud in this school, the ever-present Sarbanes–Oxley Act of 2002 had everyone in the accounting business on red alert. Even if your school is not required to do so, it is a good exercise for any principal to go through. If there is any cash exchanged in your school or any fees collected, the analysis will heighten your awareness and help you identify where and how fraud could be committed on your campus…and it could happen. People are putting their faith in you. It is your job to run a tight ship, eliminate sources of temptation, and inspire ethical behavior.

Once your faculty and staff are in place, watch for employees who believe rules do not apply to them. Your first clue to future ethical violations may be minor blips that appear more annoying than anything else. When this happens, you or someone on your staff has to take valuable time away from other important matters to deal with the situation, and the person called on the carpet often appears perturbed and self-defensive, making you feel more like the big bad wolf than an impartial school head. The offender usually has excuses: "I parked in the visitor's space because I had so many things to carry in for my class project and knew you wouldn't mind"; "Yes, I read the dress code that says 'no jeans,' but, really, you know this is who I am"; or "Sure, I got the second notice that my transcript from college has not been located in my personnel file, but, honestly, I have been too busy to get to this."

Don't fall for the explanations and excuse the behavior. Give these rascals a second chance to rectify the situation as soon as possible, make mental note of the incident and the attitude, and then watch for any future signs of rule bending. The ethical bar must be set high in your school, and everyone must be accountable. It is part of your job to see that this is done.

Presidents, heads of state, politicians, CEOs, religious leaders, and heads of schools have been leveled at one time or another and humiliated publicly by unethical practices or immoral behavior. Popeye's mission was moral righteousness, and his muscles were his secret. So too must your ethical muscle be in your leadership. Don't expect it to be there when you need it in a real emergency if you haven't flexed it and used it frequently. Muscles atrophy or grow in a person by choice. You choose how you want to live, and lead with that intention.

Seven

Honoring the Leadership Position

ACCEPTING THE ROLE

A leader is selected in some way. Either those in power identify who is to lead, or the people themselves elect the leader by formal vote or by informal agreement. By notice of sheer numbers alone, the one versus the group, a leader leads a life of privilege and power. A narcissist abuses privilege; an altruist respects privilege. A tyrant wields power; a visionary shares power. When you agree to be a principal, you are saying more than "I agree to educate children in this school to the best of my ability and to abide by the terms of my contract"; you are saying, "Yes, I will honor the leadership position with all of the unwritten expectations that go with the title." Your followers are assuming that you understand and accept these essential conditions of a leader's job. A competent leader makes a conscious effort to avoid polarization, so try your best to avoid "we-they" thinking. Principals who fall into this trap will have a hard time bringing a community together. The kindergarten teachers like one reading series, the first-grade teachers want another, and neither group wants to bend. The school forbids students to use cell phones during the academic day, and parents protest this policy, saying they have a right to talk to their children. The school board wants to close a school after it has been on probation for several years for failing to meet state academic and dropout standards, and the members of the local community are irate.

In each of these cases, and in most situations in schools where a we-they mentality is tempting, the principal has to rise above the fray and be the one to help everyone identify the issues and consider the best solutions for students. This takes self-control and focus. In complex or tense situations, it may help to follow Ronald A. Heifetz and Marty Linsky's suggestion to get a "balcony perspective." In *Leadership on the Line*, they describe a simple and unique way of looking at things that requires a leader to remove him or herself from the action briefly and look down on it to gain a better perspective. The analogy they use is a dance floor. While you are there, you see the dancers near you, feel the beat of the music, and you are part of the flow. When you leave the dance floor and look down from the balcony, you see things differently. Their theory is that a leader must move back and forth from the dance floor to the balcony, from participant to observer, to make informed and wise decisions.

When you accept the role of leader, you must understand the nuances of power. Of course, you have become familiar with the organizational chart in your school and school system, but that is only the beginning. You have to delve deeper and discover what you can about the individuals in positions of power and how their relationships can affect your school. In Dick's school, it was fairly uncomplicated. His school was in a small district where the respected long-term superintendent, Howard, called all of the shots. Dick didn't mind, at least he knew how to play the hand—please Howard. In Jim's school, it was entirely different; the power lines crackled constantly with messages moving back and forth between significant players. The nationally recognized superintendent, the well-educated and well-heeled parents on the school board, and the teachers' union all played roles in Jim's principalship. He had to become aware of any shifts of power while remaining focused on his main goal of bringing a quality education to the children in his building.

In Connie's faith-based school, one would expect power issues to be minimal. Who could not get along with others in a house of God? Apparently, religious schools are not immune to power struggles either. Sadly, Connie discovered too late that whenever a church and a school share space and people, battles often erupt over finances and power. Who pays for the construction of the playground and the costumes for the Christmas program? How much, if anything, does the church contribute to the school's annual budget? Who has the deciding vote on a school head's contract? Connie, like so many other heads in faith-based schools, learned the hard way— that the minister, priest, or rabbi, as well as the vestry, the board of directors, and the local diocese can exert tremendous pressure on a principal. Spend the bulk of your time tending to your own nest, but don't be naïve; there are always bigger birds swooping overhead.

You know that you will have issues to face as a principal, and you pray that the problems will be distinguishable and the solutions simple, but, in truth, you have to learn to deal with ambiguity. School heads who expect a clear path with easy answers will be frustrated. During your leadership, you will experience doubt and uncertainty. There will be forks in the road that will halt your steady charge until you figure out what path to take, and even then you may wonder if you have chosen well. Listening to other interpretations, giving serious thought to the matter, and then pressing on is really all you can do. Folding is not an option.

In trying to lead wisely, look beyond your own campus and district or membership group and view the other educational options in your locale. Schooling in past decades was more predictable. There were public neighborhood schools, a smattering of parochial schools, particularly in cities, connected to parish churches, and some high-end private schools for those with deep pockets. Today, we see charter schools formally recognized by the public system, learning academies headed by profit-making groups, evangelical church schools, nonprofit schools for special-needs students, and parent co-ops assisting homeschooled children. Furthermore, these new players in the educational milieu constantly shift. A charter school announces its creation with enthusiasm today, and another one closes tomorrow. A private school springs up in a town and quickly becomes successful while another one nearby struggles to stay alive. This shift in school choice demonstrates the educational ambiguity we are all dealing with in America. A school leader today does not fit into a clear niche, nor does our notion of what makes a school. As a principal, you must explore this most basic ambiguity, and look at your school and others candidly. Don't get smug; most schools have strengths to share.

Consider what other school options are offering that you are not. In *The Ambiguity Advantage, What Great Leaders Are Great At*, author David J. Wilkinson writes, "The individuals who can truly find the advantage in ambiguity are leading the way; they are the new music-makers. They are the ones exploring and creating new worlds. They inherently comprehend that these new worlds of ever increasing change, are worlds of complexity and ambiguity. These emerging breeds of leaders are becoming the new movers and shakers, with their 'song's new numbers' and new world thinking, who use ambiguity to create real advantage for themselves and their organizations."

A leader's life is one of relationships. People will look at you in wonderment or dismay and also look up to you for support and inspiration. Face it—you live in a fishbowl. It really doesn't matter if your school has two hundred or two thousand students; you are a celebrity in the community. This can be a blessing and a curse. It is nice to feel you belong to a neighborhood where people know your name and care about you. On the other hand, it is hard to go into the grocery store for a few forgotten items at dinner time and then emerge forty-five minutes later after being captured by several parents who just wanted to chat "a minute" with you. Accept this inconvenience; it is human nature to want to know about the people in leadership roles in a community. Joy, a maverick middle-aged woman who was the sole teacher, nurse, janitor, counselor, and principal in a one-room island school, was mortified to discover soon after she arrived that many people in the town knew when she had a package from L.L. Bean arrive by boat from the mainland. A day or two later, comments would flood in, complimenting her new attire. There was no privacy there, but this good-natured jack-of-all-trades educator accepted the new fishbowl life, as school leaders must. School leaders are held to a higher standard of behavior because those who deal with children's lives must be above suspicion in all things. One beer too many downed at the local pub, an inappropriate gesture made to a colleague, or a cutting comment said to a student will not be brushed off by the public. They expect more, and they should.

Many of your relationships will be with the parents of your students. In honoring the leadership position, you must understand parental angst. When children are suffering in some way, caring parents suffer more. They just can't help it. Your job as a principal is to keep that in mind as you deal with parents who are hostile, demanding, annoying, or depressed. Start any discussion by acknowledging their strong feelings about the situation, which are certainly understandable, since they are their children's best advocate. Once this is stated in a respectful and calm manner, parents usually take a deep breath, step back, and are then ready to address the problem with you. Without this preamble, you will just be spinning your wheels, and the children's issues won't get the teamwork they deserve.

In this sacred relational position in the school, accept that the principal is viewed as the spiritual leader. This is a reality in public schools as well as in nondenominational private schools. This does not mean a religious leader tied to a specific belief or practice, as in a faith-based school, but a spiritual leader as in one who cares for and nourishes those in the community in an authentic and loving way. Because of the separation of church and state in the United States, and the possibility of crossing this line, colleges and universities as well as school systems and boards rarely address the spiritual role of the school principal. What happens, however, is that in the day-to-day life of a school, the principal is expected to fill this function. As principal, you may become a counselor to a faculty member who has been abused or abandoned by a spouse. You may have to tell an employee of a tragic automobile accident where a family member has been killed and help find support for the family. You may be asked to be a pallbearer at a teenager's funeral. Diseases are part of any community, so you may be the one to make hospital or hospice visits to see a student, staff member, or a parent. National crises and local emergencies require the principal to be the spokesperson for the school, to put the event in some bearable context, and to inspire the rest of the community to respond. Emerging and established principals need to embrace this nondisclosed spiritual leadership role because, while it may not appear to be tied to school achievement, it is at the core of supporting people. Teachers and staff members who are nurtured in times of need most often become strong instructional leaders and dedicated employees. With students, it is even more basic. They engage in the learning process and achieve, or not, depending upon how they are treated.

You are the welcome wagon and the good neighbor all rolled into one. It goes with the position of school leader; therefore, greet strangers and new neighbors as potential friends. Remember how you felt like a foreigner when you entered an unfamiliar environment. You looked around nervously for a friendly face or a kindly guide. Everyone goes through this awkwardness at one time or another. As a leader, you need to perfect the initial step of connecting with people. Effective principals manage to make strangers and friends feel a part of something greater than themselves, which enables the work of schooling to get done. Be sure to touch base with other key leaders in the community such as the fire chief, police chief, or the officers who serve your area. Reach out to local ministers, priests, and rabbis. Introduce yourself to elected political leaders without pledging allegiance to them; as a principal, you need to remain politically neutral, at least in public. Get to know neighborhood businesses near school. Join a community organization such as the Chamber of Commerce. All of you are serving the same extended family and can be a resource to each other. At a moment's notice, you may have to rely on each other in order to work together quickly to support a family in need or to serve the community in crisis.

Once you have gotten over the euphoria that you felt when you heard you had been chosen to lead a school, your next reaction should be respect for the position. People respect a principal who respects the title. This critical relationship is really crucial for any employee or supervisor in the workplace, but it is often ignored. Basic attitudes and behaviors are hard to hide. A principal who recognizes the significant role and actually shows reverence for the position causes people to notice and nod approvingly. A leader needs this confirmation before any change is possible.

As principal, you may have a leadership team to assist you, a supervisor to keep you on track and evaluate your performance, coworkers to join you in the process, and families to be part of your day-to-day routine; however, a mentor can add extra seasoning to the mix. Make yourself inviting to a mentor. Contrary to what many people think, in most cases, you do not choose a mentor; a mentor chooses you! This makes sense when you realize what a true mentor can do for you; it is a generous gift that cannot be measured. Mentors take you under their wings and teach you what they know. It is not a relationship entered into lightly because it demands a significant investment of time—something that successful people place a high value on. There is also a bit of gambling tossed in the mix. Mentors surmise that you as a mentee may have potential, and, thus, they are willing to lend their name to yours as you climb up the ladder. So how does a school head get chosen? In some school systems, a new principal is automatically given a senior staff member who will be a shadow and offer counsel for a period of time. While this system is sensible, it does not happen nearly often enough. Retired school heads may volunteer to shepherd a new person, however, this too is random. First, a new principal needs to be perceptive enough to know how valuable it would be to have a mentor, and then the school head must find ways to be visible and attractive to possible mentors. There is a subtlety here. You don't want to advertise; you want to be inviting. You do this by being your best self, by attending meetings for the district or the diocese and being engaged. You do this by volunteering when there is a need for committee members. You do this by sending notes of thanks to presenters. You want to attract someone who will inspire you, and you want the mentor to feel a sense of satisfaction for enabling another school leader to grow. If the stars are aligned and sincerity is present, this relationship can enrich the lives of both mentee and mentor significantly.

LOOKING INWARD

A principal who honors the leadership position does more than give a quick nod to the ramifications of the post. You want to be among those distinguished school leaders who really make an effort to be the best they can be for the organization and for themselves. These are the principals who, by looking inward, are able to bring a community together and energize everyone to engage in learning. When you value the leadership position, you act accordingly. Practice graciousness. This does not come easily for many people, perhaps because they have not had good role models, but, for a school leader, it is essential. Outward signs often show more of the inner person than words do. Being gracious in any context shows you care, and you must care to be a distinguished principal.

Mary worked in a low-income public school in the Northeast, and it was obvious to everyone who saw her in her tailored navy blue suit with matching pumps and heard her clearly articulated speech that she was not part of the community. This initial reaction to her person didn't bother Mary one bit. She knew why she was there—to educate the children in the most caring way possible, so she just kept moving forward one child at time, one adult at a time, treating each person with utmost respect and kindness. Her instinctive graciousness made all the difference in this school. Gradually her outward appearance mattered little to the community. Families appreciated the way Mary related to everyone, and children began to enjoy school and learning.

Consider other behaviors that honor the leadership position. At all costs, you want to stay cool while remaining human. Tantrums are for two-year-olds, not principals. When feelings begin to overwhelm, have a routine in place. Take deep breaths, say, "Let me get back to you on this," close (not slam) your door and focus on another task, or go for a short walk around the building. Never raise your voice or send an e-mail in anger. Let feelings subside, and read that e-mail the next day. If someone else is out of control, don't permit yourself to join in. Say, "Let's discuss this later when you are more composed." Principals are constantly under pressure, but, bear in mind, it is how they handle the pressure that matters.

Now mull over your meeting etiquette. Manners do make the man or woman in any setting. Remember not to talk with your neighbor during a presentation. Make sure at discussion time that you are listening more than speaking, and if you are using a laptop to take notes, really take notes. Don't read e-mails or play solitaire. A high-profile public-school principal, despite his school's stellar reputation, lost the respect of his professional colleagues in the district over time because at every meeting he would sit in the back of the room during command performances for principals, ignore everyone and everything, and focus on his laptop. By this meeting behavior, he placed himself above everyone else, even if it were not conscious. The effect, however, is the same. When people appear insensitive and ego-centric, you instinctively don't want to follow their lead.

To honor the leadership position, think about how you represent yourself through your speech. A principal is constantly being observed. How ideas and feelings are expressed can greatly influence followers and standards in the school. When speaking, use proper English, and work on any bad habits that you may have developed as a student. "Hey, guys" is not a good introduction to your new faculty. Succumbing to "Valley speak" and inserting the word "like" before every phrase may be the norm for fourteen-year-olds but not for principals. Four- or five-letter "street" words flung about casually on college campuses are not OK coming from a school head, even in private meetings. Get your subjects and verbs to agree, and watch misplaced pronouns. One teacher thanked a retiring school head who taught her that words ending in "ing" needed to be pronounced that way, and, thus, the students began to hear "going" not "goin'" from this teacher. You never know the extent of your influence as a school head, and, bear in mind, that the term "head of school" comes from the British concept meaning "head teacher." If you are good, you are always teaching.

Dress as the professional you are. The specifics of dress will vary depending on climate and culture. Becky, a principal in the wilds of Alaska, wears a parka and boots to school, while Rick, a principal in Virginia, wears a tie and jacket as is expected for male principals in many city and suburban schools. Women have to be more circumspect than their male counterparts. Fashion does not always complement work in schools. A too-short skirt or a top that shows cleavage are not appropriate for any female principal on the job. Impeccable grooming is a must for all principals and says more to the public than any outfit can.

While it may seem awkward at first, you want to accept compliments courteously. Sometimes a leader who is selfless to the core will mistakenly believe that it is somehow wrong to accept a compliment, and, when one is given, will reply red-faced, "It was nothing." Well, it was enough to make another person notice. To dismiss a compliment is disingenuous and deflates the compliment giver. It is far better to acknowledge this kindness directly and say, "Thank you; I was honored to receive the award." If the congratulations are really owed to a committee, this is your chance to make it clear that a group effort enabled the success, saying something like, "Thank you. At Clearwater High, we are so appreciative of the PTA volunteers and the work they did beautifying our campus. It is lovely, isn't it?"

In honoring the leadership position, learn from your mistakes and the mistakes of others. If you know you failed, analyze how and why to prevent something similar happening again. Watch other people in positions of power, and see how they handle or don't handle mistakes made. If you do make a mistake, apologize. It will calm troubled waters, and people will respect you for being genuine.

As a school leader, you must stay informed and extend your scope beyond your own school. Many unsuccessful principals are myopic, believing the world is circumscribed by their building's walls. To resist this tendency, change your reading focus from time to time so you can cover various areas of education. Subscribe to different magazines each year to help you stay current. Interesting readings can be found in the *New York Times* periodic educational supplements and *Education Week*. For an excellent review of articles from respected publications, check out the weekly *Marshall Memo* (www.marshallmemo.com). This electronic newsletter will do much of your general scanning, and then if you want to follow up on some topic of interest, you can access the entire article.

EXEMPLIFYING BEST PRACTICES

Extraordinary leaders don't rely on charisma; they employ proven and practical ways of functioning that serve them well and stimulate others to follow their lead. Daily routines define who you are and what you value. For all leaders, simple things set the stage for greatness. Get to meetings on time. That shows basic human respect for others. It has been observed that people who are habitually late are actually egocentric; they believe that they set the clock and the action. Whether the meeting is with the school board or the safety patrols, be punctual. Write thank-you notes. An outspoken parent once remarked to a principal that handwritten notes were the best, and she was correct, but even an e-mail is better than the spoken word because writing it down shows effort and gives the writer time to choose words carefully. Most importantly, the written word permits the reader to reread the message. People tend to think of thank-you notes as responses to receiving a gift. Expand the idea of thank-you notes to include thanking people for their presence, ideas, time, and their kindness. In a school community, you cannot thank people enough. Remember that you need them.

Return phone calls and e-mails within twenty-four hours. As a principal, your phone log and inbox will be full each day. One eager young principal felt she had to get back to everyone, including a publishing company that was pushing a spelling program and another that wanted to promote student planners. With that level of expectation, her work never was finished. So use common sense—skip the sales calls but get back to everyone else promptly. Office experts recommend that CEOs check e-mails only twice a day in order to get work done. That is your decision. E-mail is a great tool, but it can be addictive if you let it rule your life. A smart school leader will scan calls and e-mails early on to see if there are any critical messages that require immediate attention and then save the rest of the responses for the end of the day. Bear in mind that a major complaint from parents is that their phone calls and e-mails are not returned at all or are not returned in a timely fashion. When this happens, anger builds and you have an additional issue to handle, perhaps greater than the original concern.

Embody correct English when writing. Principal prep programs rarely mention the vast amount of writing that a principal is required to do. Even for an English major, it can be overwhelming at times. Have a favorite handbook of English usage at your side to check on complicated subject-verb agreement or acceptable word usage. Never send out a memo, report, letter, or anything in writing without having it read by an able proofreader who will always pick up errors. It is easier to spot mistakes in someone else's work than your own. Besides basic grammar, punctuation, and spelling slipups, a good reader will let you know when the message in general or a phrase in particular is fuzzy. Whereas a store that sells tires that can afford to make an occasional blunder on its marquee, a school's product is education, so its messages should be as perfect as possible. It doesn't take much to make a reader raise an eyebrow upon seeing a mistake. After two weeks of classes, a suburban school serving an educated parent body posted this message on the electronic sign outside of the building in big bold print, "Students good job coming back. Parents you done good too." This Blue Ribbon School's communication that was intended to be complimentary turned out crass. As a head of school, you will notice grammatical errors made by your students, faculty, and staff that will be hard to ignore if you are in the business of education. With students, you can correct these by seizing the moment and teaching a lesson to a group, being careful not to humiliate any individual. With adults, take them aside quietly and privately and show them the error, teach them the right way to speak, and then explain that this kind of mistake is important to correct for their careers and for the students who are listening to them. Today, more and more people confuse the use of subjects and objects in a sentence: "Me and Connor are going to the library" needs to be corrected, even if the correction has to come from you.

Just as your writing delivers a specific message about you as a person and the school you are leading, so too does your speech. Everyone is born with a distinctive voice quality that can range from a rich reassuring baritone to an irritating, high-pitched squeal. You can't do too much about your basic sound, but you can work on your delivery. Frances Hesselbein, the former National Executive Director of the Girl Scouts and a recognized leadership coach, writes, "I feel passionately about how I express myself. Language is the greatest motivating force. You can phrase something positively and inspire people to do their best, or negatively and make them feel worried, uncertain, and self-conscious." Hesselbein believes that "the voice is the outer manifestation of the speaker's essence," so she pays attention to her tone and her pace when she speaks. One of the hardest things is to hear one's own voice. Try taping a report you must deliver to get a glimpse of how you sound, and then be serious about breaking any bad habits.

Perhaps the most significant attribute for a leader is knowing how to listen. You must listen with your whole self. A wise man once said, "Listening is not preparing a comeback." When you really listen, you hear the words, feel the inflection, and get a glimpse into the heart of the speaker. The urge to fill silent spaces should be avoided as well as the tendency to jump in with advice or "me too" comments. Most people are so often ignored that what they really want is just a listening ear. Sometimes in schools this is all it takes to solve a problem. When you are having a conference with a child, an employee, or a parent, be sure you are not interrupted for a specified time. A true emergency will require attention, but, aside from that, take no phone calls, stay seated, don't sneak a look at your watch, and honor this sacred listening time.

In order to relate to other better, learn to tell meaningful stories. Narratives tend to frame messages in ways that are both entertaining and memorable. When a principal moved from an East Coast school to a Southwest school, she didn't just tell people it was "a leap of faith." She told the story of the journey and of the people who helped her along the way. One was a Texas-sized cabbie who was squeezed into the front seat of his yellow cab and upon hearing that she was arriving alone, admitted he could never do such a thing. Shaking his head at this anomaly, he said, "Golly, I could never leave my mama." Since he was in his fifties, "mama" had to be in her seventies. Worried about his passenger, this kind man extended his card to a total stranger and said, "Call me for anything"—what true hospitality. Other guides surfaced as well. The board chairman took her and her three suitcases with all of her belongings to an unseen furnished studio apartment, which had been selected by strangers and made welcoming by people who cared. Over and over again, the friendliness of the natives amazed her, and she shared her reactions to this new place to anyone who would listen. Years later, tales of the compassionate cab driver and the three suitcases in tow were recounted by many in the community. It made them feel a part of the dream and proud of their city and school.

Part of a leader's role is to serve as a clearinghouse of information. Because of your post, information will be given to you by many means. Your job is to take time to review this information and then pass it on as you see fit to employees or groups in the school. New principals may be overwhelmed by the mass of material that arrives daily and wonder what in the world to do with all of it. The trash can or recycling bin is tempting. Instead, do a quick scan and throw out the obvious junk and then make a pile to review later. With the demands of each day, this pile can soon get out of date if you do not schedule a time at the end of the day or every other day to go through the collection to see if there is something of worth for your school to consider. Principals who neglect to do this will soon find themselves only operating in the present, putting out fires, not planting new trees. Most of the things sent will be for upcoming events and will require future planning. Browsing through publications, flyers, and invitations may make you feel guilty—what if someone comes in your office and you are not doing real work? Assuage your guilt—this is real work.

GRASPING THE ESSENCE

An insightful leader understands that he is at best a tenant farmer. His job is to till the soil, sow the seeds, and get things to grow, all the while knowing that the space is not his to claim as his own. He pays for the right to farm by the sweat of his brow and the work of his hands. Tenancy always comes with conditions: conditions of performance and conditions of time. Presidents, elected officials, corporate executives, and principals are expected to lead a nation, a state, a company, or a school toward excellence and do so with diligence, honesty, and grace.

Performance is measured by goals set and goals reached while considering the path taken to get there. Questions will always simmer in the minds of some followers. What short cuts were taken? Whose toes were stepped on? Why was this direction deemed the right one? And when will these decisions come back to haunt us? Constituents are wary by nature, but even hardened "show me" skeptics want to believe that their chosen leader is worthy of the title. The last thing anyone wants is to be embarrassed by their leader's behavior. When this happens, as it can in all arenas, progress in an organization slows to a crawl, and everyone suffers.

Conditions of time vary from post to post and person to person. Some leadership positions for elected officials are clearly spelled out for terms of office. Other positions depend upon the whim of the voters or the decision-makers. It is rare indeed for a leadership role to be free of time constraints. Don't take your post for granted; it can be whisked away in a flash. When a school leader makes the decision to leave a school, good feelings usually abound. Generally, appreciation is extended for a job well done, and there are smiles all around. Occasionally, there is a collective sigh of relief that a person has made the wise choice to depart before being asked to shape up or move on. Then there are the painful circumstances where a school head's contract is not renewed or a principal is asked to leave midyear. Many reasons real and imagined create this scenario. Parents may have sent endless complaints to the central office or board. Faculty and staff turnover may seem excessive. Achievement scores, attendance records, and graduation rates may be dismal. Financial mismanagement may be suspected. Personal indiscretions may be identified. Or a power struggle may be going on behind the scenes, and the school leader is merely the scapegoat. This line of thinking may seem peculiar for a principal moving into a new position; however, remember that for every entrance, there is an exit.

So whether your departure will be of your own doing or an actual dismissal, hold your head high and exit with grace. This sage advice was given by a successful superintendent to a group of educators in a doctoral program. When you find yourself leaving a principal post after one year or ten years, act with these things in mind: to exit with grace means burning no bridges; keeping your ego in check; thanking everyone in the community for their help and support; extending gratitude to the leadership team, trustees, or the school board for their partnership; and working until the last day with gusto so as to leave the place in good shape for the next leader. This may sound easy if you think you will find yourself leaving a position of your own accord. The real test of leadership is exiting with grace under any circumstance.

Executive coach Scott Eblin remarked that "what got you there doesn't keep you there." There is so much common sense in this statement. School leaders are hired on speculation. Usually a comprehensive search takes place when a school head is sought, but the whole experience is based on promise, even if the principal has experience in another school. People change, lives change, and each school is distinct. With every new position, you begin again. Once you are hired, you have to produce over and over again, and while mistakes may be tolerated, your track record has to be fairly solid to gain respect and really earn the title of "school leader."

Your energy and optimism blessed by fortuitous timing will help you lead well. Jeanne began her educational career in a junior high school and then became an academic dean in a faith-based coeducational high school where students and parents respected her. After a change in that school's leadership, she rejoined the public-school system and in time was appointed director of a middle-school magnet program for advanced academics. When the school district decided to open an all-girls high school, Jeanne was selected from a large pool of applicants to head the school, which was to start with grade six and eventually go through grade twelve. Now, she, the faculty, and the young women in the school are thriving in this alternative setting whose mission is to reach out to girls from economically disadvantaged backgrounds and steer them toward college. To those who had not watched this leadership ascent up close, the rise may have appeared to be random, but the truth was that Jeanne had energy to spare, and she channeled it creatively, and her optimism propelled people to action. With the appointment of her current post, timing was on her side. The district was searching for ways to increase academic achievement, increase self-esteem, and build leadership capacity in young women. Jeanne had been preparing for this position without even knowing that it would be available at some point in time by continuing to produce again and again in each job she held.

Influence is a quicksilver commodity that is hard to define in a leader. You know it when you see it, but you may wonder, "What is it worth?" John Maxwell, the prolific creator of leadership texts, states it succinctly, "Leadership is influence—nothing more, nothing less." Certainly leaders can use their powers of influence in negative or evil ways—history reminds us of this vividly—but here the emphasis is on how school leaders can use their influence in productive ways to bring out the best in people and provide an education of merit for all students. One way to nurture your potential influence is to respect, listen to, and be present for everyone in the school community, not just the top dogs. When you do this, your influence grows. This approach requires day-to-day and minute-to-minute vigilance on your part so that you can be true to your intentions and keep the top dogs' barking at bay. Another way to expand your sphere of influence is to be honest in all of your dealings and communications. Morris was known in his school and his district as a master spin doctor. At times, colleagues marveled at his skill in getting of them out of jams, and the central office relaxed a bit when he had to explain "a happening" at his high school to the press. Over time, however, this talent of framing the "truth" to fit his needs began to erode the faith people had in his leadership and the school. To those who came to realize that this essential leadership trait was missing, he became a fraud. To be a leader of lasting influence, you must be able to distinguish between what is superficial and what is real, and then speak this truth to others. Authentic influence never smacks of manipulation or coercion. It is pure, not contrived or self-serving, and sets a person apart as a leader worthy of following.

Being asked to serve as a leader should inspire awe at your responsibility. Accept the invitation graciously, and vow to honor the position. Be earnest about the endeavor you are undertaking as a school leader, and consider the gravity of the role. People will be depending on you as a principal to change their lives in some way. Stay focused on the task at hand—education—and don't let petty annoyances, power, or prestige get in your way. Be clear in your own mind that the deference coming your way is due to the position, not to you as a person. This important distinction, if left unheeded, can defeat even the most promising of leaders. It is the presidency, the governorship, and the headship that inspires respect. The individual in that position is merely an occupant who must do his best to be worthy of the title. Grasping the weightiness of this matter requires routine reflection, which will lead to eventual wisdom.

Conclusion

Parents and communities are clamoring for improvements in schools. Moreover, businesses are eager to hire well-educated, responsible workers who will help their companies thrive. Despite many attempts over the last decades to increase student learning by focusing on curriculum, instruction, and assessment, specifically by using state-mandated testing, many of our schools are still struggling. Parents are dismayed, teachers are frustrated, and students often appear disengaged in the learning process. We must continue to delve into these essential components of schooling, but we also need to address a critical factor in a school's success, one that has been ignored by many, and that is the role of the principal. As in any organization, the person at the top, whether it is a CEO or a head of school, is the one who makes things happen. Vision, know-how, and the ability to bring people together to work toward a common goal is what a leader does. If he or she does these things well, people grow, and corporations, organizations, and schools prosper. If the leader does not have the essential skills, then businesses, associations, and schools fail. And when a school fails, all of society suffers—students, parents, teachers, and communities—not just for today but for tomorrow. When this happens, dreams die, education levels decline, earning power is diminished, and the cycle of dependency and poverty continues.

There are people with insight who are beginning to bring this issue to the forefront of education in meaningful ways. It is coming from various avenues such as the research that is occurring at the Wallace Foundation and certain initatives from lawmakers and leadership organizations. Perhaps teachers are our best source of information for what makes a school successful. They tell us, if we would listen, what they have known all along, that it is the principal, the person at the top, who inspires them to do their best work so the students can learn.

Will Miller, president of the Wallace Foundation writes, "We [also] commission research on school leadership. In the largest of these studies, covering 180 schools in nine states, researchers from the University of Minnesota and the University of Toronto concluded, 'We have not found a single case of a school improving its student achievement record in the absence of talented leadership." (New York Times OP-Ed Contributer, April 17, 2015. "Want Reform? Principals Matter Too.")

So what are next steps? It is clear that various groups must acknowledge that the school leader is essential to a school's success and student learning. And then stakeholders need to jump on board and vigorously do their part, working within their own sphere of responsibility and in collaboration with one other.

Colleges and universities can take this opportunity to examine their programs of studies for principal candidates and novice principals. A few academic institutions have made significant improvements, but not nearly enough preparation programs are considered effective. Depth, breadth, and innovation are necessary. Most principals come from the teaching profession; however, the role of a school head is vastly different and that fact must be addressed. Preparation programs should include the usual scope of requirements such as policy, finance, law, curriculum, instruction and assessment, and should also focus on how to be an agent of change; how to manage data and get meaning from it; how to create a collaborative culture for belonging, learning, and leading; how to work with communities; how to design an effective organization; how to set a vision and communicate it to others; and how to internalize lessons learned from the leadership field in general. Aspiring school heads moving up from lower-level administrative posts such as deans or department chairs needs this same shoring up in order to be effective in their new roles as principals. At charter schools and for profit schools, inexperienced educational administrators who may have come from the business world require a similar intensive program of studies in order to serve their schools and their students well.

The *how* is as important as the *what* in developing exemplary principals. Surely, the program of studies will include listening to lectures given by recognized experts and reading books on theory and practice, but it should also incorporate dialogue with experienced school heads, researchers in the field, and leadership experts from other disciplines. It should be full of team projects designed to gain practice in solving real school problems with others. It should value observation and set up a schedule for visiting schools of excellence and seeing principals who shine. It should foster intimate study groups where emerging leaders can debate issues and help each other define ethics, policies, and practices of their own. It should encourage introspection and reflective experiences such as writing in journals and engaging in deep conversations that get to the core of one's own strengths and weaknesses, and the challenge of being a principal who can truly make a difference in the lives of children and adults in a school community. This book, *The Principal's Chair: Who Sits There Matters, A Secret of School Success* could be a catalyst and could promote these meaningful conversations that help mold mature school leaders.

People and organizations charged with hiring school leaders have a significant role to play in finding the right person to do the job. In various structures of schooling this is done a bit differently, yet the challenge is the same. Superintendents and school boards of public schools have this important task. For independent schools, search committees, sometimes supported by headhunters, do the initial work, and then a board of trustees selects the new head. In some cases, a diocese, church, or umbrella organization has the ultimate vote or veto power. One would hope that in all of these situations, there is serious debate about the school's needs and the leadership skills necessary to move the school forward. Furthermore, the search requires attention and participation from various community members, so inclusion should be part of the hiring protocol, even though the final decision rests in the hands of a few. Basic requirements of education and experience should be noted, although the search cannot end there. References must be secured by talking to previous employers in some detail to gain a real sense of the candidate applying for the job. An unbiased person should do this key work. Finding an educator with the right professional and personal profile to lead a school takes time. Decisions made in a hurry often harm a school in the future. For superintendents, school boards, boards of trustees, and other significant players, choosing a school head may be the most salient duty that they ever perform in their post.

Membership organizations and accrediting agencies are designed to support schools and their leaders. For any principals, but especially for novice school heads, these groups can significantly affect a school leader's ability to lead a school well. Because they realize their potential to help principals and improve education for schools, many organizations require or offer seminars for new school heads or continuing education in specialized fields. It would be advantageous if regional, state, and national organizations would look to the needs of their school leaders and find ways to fill some of these gaps, perhaps in collaboration with colleges and universities. Even when a principal has the credentials to lead, the challenge to do so continues. Often, the school head receives the least amount of professional development in a school community. In addition, accrediting agencies, both state and private ones, must be rigorous in setting standards of educational requirements for school leaders and schools as well as conscientious in their regular reviews of a leader's performance and a school's efficacy.

Once hired, the principal is the one who takes the lead, assessing the school's landscape, determining what needs to be done and how, and defining the vision and communicating it to the community. Realizing that he or she has the opportunity to help students excel at life should be empowering and humbling at once. Recognizing that a school head also has the responsibility to grow adults should be the impetus for setting and monitoring instructional goals for teachers and refining interpersonal relationships for all adults on campus. Intentionality and integrity should drive all of the principal's efforts. Honoring the leadership position is what sets mediocre principals apart from great ones. These outstanding school leaders find satisfaction and even joy in the myriad tasks of the job, knowing that they can never settle for what is and must constantly seek ways to improve lives. They focus their energy on helping everyone be the best they can be, understanding that as leaders, they define the path for student success and model commitment and the pursuit of excellence each step along the way.

Bibliography

Allen, David. *Getting Things Done: The Art of Stress-Free Productivity*. New York: Penguin, 2001.

Collins, Jim. *Good to Great: Why Some Companies Make the Leap…and Others Don't*. New York: HarperCollins, 2001.

Covey, Stephen. *Principle-Centered Leadership*. New York: Fireside, 1992.

De Pree, Max. *Leadership Is an Art*. New York: Dell, 1989.

———. *Leadership Jazz*. New York: Doubleday, 1992.

George, Bill, and Peter Sims. *True North: Discovering Your Authentic Leadership*. San Francisco: Jossey-Bass, 2007.

Greenleaf, Robert K. *Servant Leadership: A Journey into the Nature of Legitimate Power and Greatness*. Mahwah, NJ: Paulist Press, 1977, 1991, 2002.

———.*The Servant Leader*. Indianapolis, IN: The Robert K. Greenleaf Center for Servant Leadership, 1991, rev. edition 2008.

Heifetz, Ronald A., and Marty Linsky. *Leadership on the Line: Staying Alive through the Dangers of Leading*. Boston: Harvard Business School Press, 2002.

Kouzes, James M., and Barry Z. Posner. *The Leadership Challenge: How To Make Extraordinary Things Happen in Organizations*. San Francisco: Jossey-Bass, 2007, 2012.

Maxwell, John C. *The 5 Levels of Leadership*: *Proven Steps to Maximize Your Leadership*. New York: Hachette Books, 2011.

———.*Developing the Leader Within You*. Nashville: Thomas Nelson, 2000.

———. *How Successful People Think*: *Change Your Thinking, Change Your Life*. New York: Hachette Books, 2009.

O'Connor, Elizabeth. *Servant Leaders, Servant Structures*. Washington, DC: The Servant Leadership School, 1991.

Pfeffer, Jeffrey. *The Knowing-Doing Gap: How Smart Companies Turn Knowledge into Action*. Boston: Harvard Business School Press, 2000.

Scharmer, Otto. *Theory U: Leading from the Future as It Emerges*. San Francisco: Berrett-Koehler, 2009.

Scharmer, Otto, and Katrin Kaufer. *Leading from the Emerging Future from Ego-System to Eco-System Economies*. San Francisco: Berrett-Koehler, 2013.

Sull, Donald, and Kathleen Eisenhardt. *Simple Rules: How to Thrive in a Complex World*. New York: Houghton Mifflin Harcourt, 2015

Taylor, Jill Bolte. *My Stroke of Insight*: *A Brain Scientist's Personal Journey*. New York: Penguin, 2008.

Useem, Michael. *The Go Point: When It's Time to Decide—Knowing What to Do and When to Do It*. New York: Three Rivers Press, 2006.

Wilkinson, David J. *The Ambiguity Advantage: What Great Leaders Are Great At*. New York: Palgrave Macmillan, 2006.

Zander, Rosamund Stone, and Benjamin Zander. *The Art of Possibilities: Transforming Professional and Personal Life*. Cambridge, MA: Harvard Business School Press, 2000.

About the Author

Judith D. Knotts is a seasoned school head, leadership expert, and writer. She is adept at combining curated theories of being a CEO with vivid and varied examples of doing or not doing an outstanding job as a school leader. With experience gleaned from decades of observing principals in action, Dr. Knotts has been a consultant to schools, a member of the National Advisory Board for the Harvard Principals' Center, and codirector of the Joan L. Curcio International Women's Leadership Conferences at Oxford University. She has served on accreditation teams for the Independent School Association of the Southwest (ISAS) and is currently a commissioner for the Texas Catholic Conference Education Department.

The signs of outstanding leadership appear primarily among the followers. Are the followers reaching their potential? Are they learning? Serving? Do they achieve the required results? Do they change with grace? Manage conflict?

—Max De Pree

R00082

Made in the USA
San Bernardino, CA
25 September 2016